4-INGREDIENT
Smoothies + Juices

4-INGREDIENT
Smoothies + Juices

100 EASY, NUTRITIOUS RECIPES FOR LIFELONG HEALTH

Dee Dine

Founder of Green Smoothie Gourmet

PAGE STREET
PUBLISHING CO.

First published in 2021 by
Page Street Publishing Co.
27 Congress Street, Suite 105
Salem, MA 01970
www.pagestreetpublishing.com

25 24 23 22 21   1 2 3 4 5

ISBN-13: 978-1-64567-229-6
ISBN-10: 1-64567-229-8

Library of Congress Control Number: 2020939443

Cover and book design by Ashley Tenn for Page Street Publishing Co.
Photography by Dee Dine

Printed and bound in China

Dedication

To my beloved family—my husband, Philip; our three girls, Alexandra, Jessica and Joelle; and our joyous pets, Peri, our Pomeranian, and Casper, our cockatiel. And to all my inspiring followers on Instagram and my blog, Green Smoothie Gourmet.

Contents

Vegetable Harvest: 115
GARDEN GREEN SMOOTHIES & JUICES

Daily Decadence: 147
DESSERT FRAPPES & SHAKES

Smoothies Transformed into Frozen Treats 177

Introduction

Hey there! I'm Dee Dine. You might know me as the creator behind Green Smoothie Gourmet, my space on the Internet where I share healthy, plant-based recipes made with few ingredients. Thank you for stepping into my world of smoothies and juices, rife with frothy fruit, pungent greens, tangy superfoods, bright spices and a large selection of chocolaty, decadent wonders, all with at least one commonality: whole-food nutrition. In this book, you'll find smoothies and juices made with only four ingredients. Yes, only four ingredients.

Smoothies and juices are the perfect element to a healthy lifestyle. First of all, they are delicious! My four-ingredient smoothies and juices are like drinking frosty sunshine or downing a decadent dessert. What a treat to know these delicious beverages are healthy. Smoothies and juices are an incredibly quick and easy way to get a nutritious boost to your health, immunity and well-being.

My minimal ingredient smoothies and juices are easy to make without taking long shopping trips and spending lots of time prepping. For instance, the 100 recipes in this book use primarily healthy, whole foods found in your pantry or grocery store. The recipes are packed with general vitamins and minerals, but each also provides nutritional support for ten target areas, including protein, energy, brain, immunity, beauty, fiber, sleep, stress, weight and mood.

I'm confident you'll feel a healthy boost after drinking even one smoothie. Drink them regularly and you'll feel terrific. Sometimes there is a quick fix!

MY PATH TO A DAILY SMOOTHIE

I adopted my smoothie-a-day lifestyle back in college, right after I failed an organic chemistry exam. The day I got my grade, I realized my overnight studying and poor eating habits were upending my education. The thought of suddenly cooking in our limited kitchen was overwhelming. And then a friend suggested smoothies. Lightbulb moment! So I bought a refurbished blender and started drinking a green smoothie every single day. Within a week, I was sleeping better, my digestion and mood felt better, my mind felt clearer—even my skin looked healthier.

Yes, I graduated, and yes, I managed to convert a few fast-food-loving roommates over to the smoothie side as well. After graduation, I continued on a path encompassing both science and journalism, so, once I had a family, it seemed like a natural move to launch a healthy recipe blog and run it full time. Cooking really is a science, so I lean heavily on my science background when developing recipes for my blog and for this book.

I choose ingredients that provide delicious flavors, of course, but also solid-state nutrition. And for nearly six years now, I have been developing minimal-ingredient recipes that target various nutritional benefits based on empirical scientific findings, found in reports by reputable entities including the National Institutes of Health and the Royal Scientific Society.

In addition to targeted nutrition, you will find my recipes accommodate dietary requirements for those who eat dairy-free, gluten-free and refined sugar-free. I worked to make my smoothies and juices appeal to children and adults and are suitable for breakfast, snacks or dessert. You'll notice as you run through my recipes a range of produce and superfoods—and a fair share of chocolate.

Welcome to my smoothie world! I can't wait to see how my recipes bring about the changes you are seeking.

Love,

Dee Dine

A SMOOTHIE & JUICE BOOK OF A DIFFERENT KIND

I structured this book to help you easily establish a nutritional smoothie and juice routine. Here is a bit about how the book is arranged and some defined terms to help before you start.

You will find six chapters color-coded to represent smoothies and juices made with leafy greens, fruit, superfoods, vegetables, desserts and smoothies as frozen desserts. Each recipe has specific nutritional benefits, targeted to help with one of the following areas:

- protein
- energy
- brain
- immunity
- beauty

- fiber
- sleep
- stress
- weight
- mood

KNOW BEFORE YOU START

Smoothies and Juices: Each smoothie and juice recipe makes two (8-oz [240-ml]) drinks.

Shots: Each shot recipe makes 4 ounces (120 ml).

Nutritional Information: The nutritional information is for one 8-ounce (240-ml) serving for smoothies and juices and one 4-ounce (120-ml) serving for shots.

Mainstream Ingredients: The ingredients are generally mainstream, with very few unusual suggestions, and all of them can easily be found at your local grocer or online.

Substitutions: Every recipe includes suggestions on how to substitute ingredients.

Pantry Items: Most recipes make use of some pantry items, which are not counted as one of the four ingredients. I am assuming you'll have them on hand. These include:

- milk
- coffee
- yogurt
- lemon juice

- ground spices
- salt
- vanilla

Many Banana-Free Recipes: Bananas are delicious, but most smoothie recipes depend on them for thickening and sweetening, so I chose to use other options in most recipes in an effort to provide recipes you won't find elsewhere.

Smoothies vs. Juices vs. Shots: Let's help you choose! Smoothies provide you with more fiber in general, and your body metabolizes smoothie nutrition more slowly, providing slow-burning energy. With little fiber to slow things down, juices provide a faster absorption of nutrition, resulting in a rapid spike of nutritional intake and energy. Shots are a concentrated juice and deliver a more potent dose.

On Canned Foods: I recommend striving to use whole, unprocessed foods when possible. They should also be familiar, such as leafy greens, berries, herbs, fruits and teas. When possible, try to use the fresh or frozen version of the ingredient. Occasionally, I recommend a canned food, such as garbanzo beans, to acquire the liquid aquafaba, and canned coconut milk. This coconut milk should be unsweetened and only coconut milk and possibly guar gum should be listed in the ingredients. I recommend the brands Thai Kitchen® and Native Forest®.

On Superfoods: There are a few less-familiar ingredients in my recipes that are sometimes called superfoods. These include spirulina, baobab, goji berries, dragon fruit and a few more. They are available online in some form, or you can swap them out if they are inaccessible to you. But I highly recommend trying to find them, as these superfoods provide well-documented physical and mental boosts. Quality brands include Navitas Organics®, Terrasoul Superfoods, Sunfood™ and Anthony's Goods.

On Milk and Ice: Many of my recipes call for milk. When I think a certain milk works best, I suggest it, often almond milk, cashew milk or coconut milk. But where the ingredient list notes only "milk," feel free to choose the milk you personally use at home. Also, several recipes call for both ice and milk. The mix of the two creates a frosty and creamy texture.

On Chocolate: Cacao powder is a nutritious raw form of cocoa powder; however, it is relatively expensive and not as easy to obtain as unsweetened cocoa powder. Still, if you can use cacao powder, it provides a higher level of all the nutritional benefits chocolate provides.

If a recipe features dark chocolate or chocolate chips, look for a brand that is at least 70% cacao and lists cocoa butter and very few other ingredients. Some quality brands include Hu Kitchen, Enjoy Life®, Chocolove and Theo Chocolate.

Fresh, Frozen or Cooked: In general, I like to work with frozen fruits and vegetables, but freshly cooked and cooled or raw vegetables work as well. Here are a few specific tips. For the creamiest results with cauliflower, steam and cool it first. To achieve a creamier texture, dates, cashews and almonds can be soaked for at least 4 hours or boiled for 5 minutes. Buy only organic zucchini; use it raw and keep the skin on. To get an up-to-date list of other produce that should be bought organic because of their propensity to absorb pesticides, check the Clean and Dirty lists put out annually by the nutritional nonprofit, EWG.org.

Meal Prep and Storage: My smoothies always taste best immediately after they are blended. That's also when they are strongest nutritionally. The second best option is to pre-prep your smoothie. Here are my two favorite ways to pre-make a smoothie:

1. Freeze the blended smoothie in ice cube trays, bag the cubes and store them in the freezer. To prepare to drink a smoothie, set 4 or 5 cubes in a jar and refrigerate the night before. Shake or blend the next morning.

2. Bag the individual ingredients, minus the liquid, in single-smoothie portions and freeze. When it is convenient for you, remove a bag, pour the smoothie contents into a blender, add the recipe's required liquid and blend.

Morning Emeralds:
LEAFY GREENS SMOOTHIES & JUICES

Leafy greens are so nutritionally valuable, we might as well call them vitamins. I'll have vitamins, tomato and onion on my sandwich please! OK, so that's not logical, but shall we list all the nutritional benefits leafy greens provide?

First of all, they are rife with B vitamins, known for boosting energy and supporting the digestive and nervous systems. They are also rich in immune-boosting vitamins A, C and E. And don't forget the magnesium that helps us fall asleep. Or the calcium that keeps our bones strong. And the omega-3s and protein that enrich our brains, among other organs.

So, it's clear we should be eating our leafy greens. The USDA suggests adults eat 2 to 3 cups of vegetables per day. But it takes 2 cups of leafy greens to equal a USDA 1-cup serving of vegetables. That's a lot of greens to eat in one day. But it's not so hard when you throw them into a smoothie. They are easily disguised by the many fruits and flavors we can add.

My favorite smoothies in this chapter include Spinach Avocado (page 16), Kale Latte (page 19) and Matcha Moon Milk (page 27). I even have a Thin Mint smoothie (page 35). Yep, mint is a leafy green. Spinach, kale, collards, bok choy, lettuces, basil and even beet greens are also leafy greens. Remember, they are not cooked when you add them to a smoothie, so rinsing them first is essential. In fact, if the pre-washed packaged greens are available to you, I would opt for those. I normally say buy fresh, but the convenience of pre-washed might mean you eat more greens. As an added bonus, those packaged greens are often the baby version, as in baby spinach or baby kale. The baby versions of these leafy greens always taste milder than non-baby versions and are a very useful option when you are trying to hide the presence of veggies. They're also easier to blend smoothly into your smoothies. Let's go blend some leafy greens!

Spinach Avocado

Leafy greens really know how to benefit skin, including vitamins that support collagen production and antioxidants that reduce the effects of aging. Combining a leafy green like spinach with nourishing avocado allows you to create a wonderfully thick milkshake texture in a smoothie that is mostly vegetables. Clever trick! Kids love most smoothies, but they seem to adore those that have pear and mango, and this one has both. The perfect smoothie for everyone.

MAKES 2 (8-OZ [240-ML]) SMOOTHIES

½ avocado, pitted and peeled

1 cup (30 g) spinach leaves

½ cup (82 g) mango chunks

½ pear, cored and chopped

1¼ cups (300 ml) almond milk

½ tsp vanilla extract

Add all the ingredients to a blender and process until the mixture is smooth. Enjoy immediately, refrigerate for 24 hours or freeze for later.

SUBSTITUTIONS: Spinach in this recipe can be replaced by baby spinach, baby kale and even romaine lettuce. The avocado and mango should not be substituted for texture. Choose Bartlett, Comice or Anjou pears; avoid crunchier pears such as Bosc and Asian.

Protein: 2.5 g | Fiber: 5.4 g | Fat: 11.6 g | Calories: 188 | Sodium: 103 mg | Carbs: 21.3 g | Sugars: 13.1 g

Kale Latte

The green grapes in this smoothie bring a fresh sweetness, the chamomile tea induces calm and the kale, the star of the day, can't even be tasted. Is that a good thing? I think it depends on who you talk to—some people want to taste the "green." If that's you, increase the kale. Otherwise, enjoy the experience of a frothy, delicious, fresh-tasting latte of a different kind. The perfect drink to enjoy just before bed.

MAKES 2 (8-OZ [240-ML]) SMOOTHIES

½ cup (33 g) kale leaves

¼ cup (38 g) green grapes

¼ cup (60 ml) chamomile tea

½ cup (120 ml) warm milk

Add all the ingredients to a blender and process until the mixture is smooth. Enjoy immediately, or if you prefer, refrigerate for an hour to give it an extra chill. Alternatively, warm the smoothie gently in the microwave.

. . . .

SUBSTITUTIONS: The kale can be replaced by mild leafy greens such as baby spinach. The grapes can be swapped for pear, but the tea can't be substituted.

Protein: 1.5 g | Fiber: 0.7 g | Fat: 0.7 g | Calories: 43 | Sodium: 53 mg | Carbs: 8.2 g | Sugars: 3.4 g

Blueberry Morning

A muffin in a glass. This smoothie is the perfect nutritious substitute for your morning blueberry muffin. The spinach is hidden behind the blueberry flavor, and the vanilla and cinnamon give you the essence of a baked muffin. Blueberries are often included in immunity-boosting recipes, and rightly so due to their high level of antioxidants. However, those same antioxidants also provide powerful support to the brain, putting a drag on deterioration from aging, and even boosting intelligence and memory functions. So, be smart and have a blueberry smoothie this morning!

MAKES 2 (8-OZ [240-ML]) SMOOTHIES

½ cup (15 g) spinach leaves

1 cup (148 g) blueberries

½ cup (120 ml) milk

½ cup (70 g) ice

½ tsp vanilla extract

½ tsp ground cinnamon

Add all the ingredients to a blender and process until the mixture is smooth. Enjoy immediately.

. . . .

SUBSTITUTIONS: The spinach can be replaced by baby spinach or baby kale. The blueberries shouldn't be substituted in a blueberry smoothie; however, the recipe would work with blackberries or raspberries.

Protein: 1.3 g | Fiber: 1.9 g | Fat: 1.5 g | Calories: 73 | Sodium: 76 mg | Carbs: 14.8 g | Sugars: 10.2 g

Chocolate Banana

I considered naming this smoothie "Spinach Chocolate Banana," but somehow it didn't have the same ring. This smoothie is remarkably delicious. One of my recipe testers, my husband, "needed" me to make it three times before he would declare it perfect. The green flavor is not evident, which is key in a leafy green smoothie. If you freeze your bananas, you won't taste the banana flavor either, it'll be all chocolate—with a touch of cinnamon meant to balance blood sugar. It's a wonderful treat to soak up leafy green energizing goodness.

MAKES 2 (8-OZ [240-ML]) SMOOTHIES

1 cup (30 g) spinach leaves

1 banana, peeled

3 tbsp (16 g) cacao powder

1 tsp ground cinnamon

½ cup (120 ml) milk

½ cup (70 g) ice

Add all the ingredients to a blender and process until the mixture is smooth. Enjoy immediately, refrigerate for 24 hours or freeze for later.

. . . .

SUBSTITUTIONS: The spinach can be replaced by mild leafy greens such as baby spinach, baby kale or even romaine lettuce. Unsweetened cocoa can be used instead of cacao powder. Or melt ¼ cup (44 g) of quality dark chocolate in the microwave at 15-second intervals. Quality chocolate brands with minimal ingredients include Enjoy Life®, Theo, Chocolove and Hu Kitchen.

Protein: 3.1 g | Fiber: 4.9 g | Fat: 2.6 g | Calories: 107 | Sodium: 84 mg | Carbs: 23.4 g | Sugars: 10.4 g

Tropical Jackfruit

I love using mixed greens in my smoothies. I know I am getting the benefits of a wide selection of greens including spinach, kale, beet greens, arugula and more. This smoothie especially boosts immunity with the use of vitamin C–strong jackfruit and coconut milk. Coconut milk is a strong anti-microbial, which means it can help the body fight germs. It is also full of anti-inflammatories, which help when the body's response to invaders gets out of control. As a bonus, the texture of coconut milk makes any smoothie thick and dreamy. With the combination of coconut, pineapple and jackfruit, this smoothie has an especially tropical air.

MAKES 2 (8-OZ [240-ML]) SMOOTHIES

½ cup (15 g) mixed leafy greens

½ cup (82 g) pineapple chunks

½ cup (82 g) jackfruit, ripe and frozen

1 cup (240 ml) coconut milk, canned

Add all the ingredients to a blender and process until the mixture is smooth. Enjoy immediately, or if you prefer, refrigerate for an hour to give it an extra chill.

SUBSTITUTIONS: The coconut milk can be replaced with coconut water if you want a lighter smoothie, but you will lose the anti-microbial power. The jackfruit can easily be replaced with frozen mango chunks.

Protein: 2 g | Fiber: 1.4 g | Fat: 20.2 g | Calories: 261 | Sodium: 58 mg | Carbs: 21.6 g | Sugars: 6.1 g

Butter Lettuce Berry

The butter lettuce in this smoothie is an undetectable green, both because of its mild flavor and the thickness of the cashews and frosty berries. But its nutritional goodness is up front and center. That's because butter lettuce provides your body with essential vitamin A, a nutrient desperately needed by your central nervous system to allow you to think, move and relax. Butter lettuce, also called Boston or Bibb lettuce, provides 70 percent of the recommended daily requirement. Butter lettuce also provides iron and calcium. Add in the calming effect of tryptophan in the cashews, and you will feel positively tranquil.

MAKES 2 (8-OZ [240-ML]) SMOOTHIES

½ cup (27 g) butter lettuce

½ cup (72 g) blackberries

½ cup (76 g) red grapes

½ cup (75 g) cashews, raw and unsalted

1 cup (240 ml) ice water

Add all the ingredients to a blender and process until the mixture is smooth. Enjoy immediately.

. . . .

SUBSTITUTIONS: The cashews can be replaced with almonds, which don't provide tryptophan, but still help relieve stress by supporting the body's serotonin production. Blueberries and raspberries can replace blackberries, and green grapes can replace the red grapes here.

Protein: 6.1 g | Fiber: 3.3 g | Fat: 16.1 g | Calories: 240 | Sodium: 7 mg | Carbs: 21.8 g | Sugars: 9.4 g

Matcha Moon Milk

Matcha Moon Milk is a spin-off of the traditional Ayurvedic drink of milk with honey, consumed at night before bed to optimize sleep. My moon milk has similar calming effects due to matcha, which is strong in L-theanine, the amino acid best associated with relieving stress, but it is best for energizing your morning. That's because matcha, the high-quality, powdered version of green tea, contains caffeine, about half that of a cup of coffee. But matcha's caffeine is metabolically programmed to be disbursed more slowly in the body than caffeine from coffee, so you'll have a gentle flow of energy all day. So energize your morning in a calmer way with my Matcha Moon Milk.

MAKES 1 (8-OZ [240-ML]) DRINK

1 cup (240 ml) milk, divided

1 tsp matcha powder

3 mint leaves, crushed

1 tbsp (15 ml) maple syrup, to taste

Add 2 tablespoons (30 ml) of milk to a mug and microwave for 15 seconds. Stir in the matcha powder until it's dissolved. Pour in the rest of the milk, add the crushed mint leaves and microwave again for 45 seconds. Taste test and stir in the maple syrup if sweetening is necessary, 1 teaspoon at a time. Enjoy immediately.

. . . .

SUBSTITUTIONS: Instead of adding matcha powder to the milk, you can steep a green tea teabag in the hot milk for 20 minutes instead, remove the bag and proceed with the recipe. However, the flavor and caffeine will be less than if you used matcha powder. When buying matcha powder, be sure to choose ceremonial grade for the best flavor; I always avoid culinary grade even when baking because of its bitter flavor.

Protein: 6.1 g | Fiber: 3.3 g | Fat: 2.5 g | Calories: 124 | Sodium: 71 mg | Carbs: 21.4 g | Sugars: 11.9 g

Watermelon Basil

A fragrant, frosty treat that is fun to eat and has the ability to help you lose fat quickly. Watermelon contains arginine, an amino acid that directs your body to focus on burning fat. The sweet melon also helps your body stay hydrated, which helps curb snack cravings. Turning watermelon into a smooth sorbet-like treat, fragrant with leafy basil and zingy with ginger, ups the experience. To ensure a dry, frosty texture, freeze chunks of watermelon first, and blend minimally.

MAKES 2 (8-OZ [240-ML]) SMOOTHIES

2 cups (300 g) watermelon, frozen

1 tbsp (6 g) ginger, peeled and grated finely

2 tbsp (5 g) fresh basil leaves, for garnish

Add all the ingredients except the basil leaves to a blender and process until the mixture is smooth. Enjoy immediately, or if you prefer, refrigerate for an hour to give it an extra chill. Serve in a glass with the fresh basil leaves.

. . . .

SUBSTITUTIONS: If you can't obtain watermelon, strawberries also pair well with basil. Other fruits that make great slushies include frozen peaches, raspberries, mango and even kiwi. And other herbs that perform well in smoothies include mint, rosemary and thyme.

Protein: 0.9 g | Fiber: 0.6 g | Fat: 0.2 g | Calories: 46 | Sodium: 2 mg | Carbs: 11.4 g | Sugars: 9.3 g

Raspberry Cooler

This beautiful rose red smoothie will raise your spirits by just staring at it for a while before drinking. But once you drink this concoction of leafy greens, raspberries and cauliflower, your body will thank you for all the healthy fiber you ingested. Although many fruits and vegetables contain fiber, raspberries are especially high in it, providing 8 grams per cup. Add to that the 3 grams per cup from cauliflower and we have a veritable fiber party going on. The leafy greens follow up with a myriad of essential vitamins and minerals. The lemon juice provides a refreshing tang.

MAKES 2 (8-OZ [240-ML]) SMOOTHIES

1 cup (100 g) cauliflower florets

½ cup (15 g) mixed leafy greens

1 cup (123 g) raspberries

2 tbsp (30 ml) lemon juice

1 cup (240 ml) ice water

For the creamiest result, first steam and cool your cauliflower. Then add all the ingredients to a blender and process until the mixture is smooth. Enjoy immediately.

. . . .

SUBSTITUTIONS: Leave out the cauliflower to reduce the fiber. Swap out raspberries for mango, which also has a good amount of fiber, about 5 grams per cup. One tip for smoothies that contain cauliflower: don't smell them in the blender. For some reason, blended cauliflower smells sour. Rest assured, however, that smell does not translate into a sour taste. In fact, adding cauliflower to a smoothie boosts nutrition and a creamy texture, yet, depending on the amount, doesn't change the flavor.

Protein: 1.3 g | Fiber: 1.5 g | Fat: 0.5 g | Calories: 48 | Sodium: 24 mg | Carbs: 3.2 g | Sugars: 1.6 g

Pear Avocado

Fiber is vital to our digestive health, heart health, blood sugar levels and even immunity protection. This smoothie is an ideal source of healthy fiber, with nearly 12 grams provided by the kale, avocado and pear. The creamy texture is largely from the avocado, as is the pretty soft green color. But honestly, the taste is all sweet and pear-like. To make this high-fiber smoothie more child-friendly, double the pear.

MAKES 2 (8-OZ [240-ML]) SMOOTHIES

½ cup (33 g) kale leaves

½ cup (75 g) avocado, pitted and peeled

1 pear, cored and chopped

1 cup (240 ml) coconut water

Pinch of ground ginger

Add all the ingredients to a blender and process until the mixture is smooth. Enjoy immediately, or if you prefer, refrigerate for an hour to give it an extra chill.

. . . .

SUBSTITUTIONS: The pear can be replaced with apples, peaches and plums. Ice water can be used instead of coconut water, and the ginger can be swapped with cinnamon.

Protein: 2.6 g | Fiber: 7.1 g | Fat: 10.1 g | Calories: 174 | Sodium: 137 mg | Carbs: 21.1 g | Sugars: 10.2 g

Apple Pie

Let's have a salad with our apple pie. Sounds ridiculous, but it works! And it's because the lettuce and tomatoes disappear behind the flavor of the apples and cinnamon. The result is a creamy smoothie that tastes like apple pie. And the nutritional gains can be seen in the mirror. Apples are known for their wrinkle-reducing antioxidants, and tomatoes provide skin-loving potassium and vitamin C, as well as the famed anti-inflammatory, lycopene. So, I hope you enjoy your pie with a side of salad.

MAKES 2 (8-OZ [240-ML]) SMOOTHIES

1 romaine lettuce leaf

1 cup (120 g) apples,
not peeled

3 cherry tomatoes

½ cup (120 ml) yogurt

½ cup (120 ml) milk

1 tsp ground cinnamon

Add all the ingredients to a blender and process until the mixture is smooth. Enjoy immediately or refrigerate for later.

. . . .

SUBSTITUTIONS: Replace the romaine with any leafy greens of mild flavor such as spinach or butter lettuce. You can adjust the amounts of yogurt and milk based on your preferences, as long as they balance out to a full cup.

Protein: 5.7 g | Fiber: 4.9 g | Fat: 2 g | Calories: 150 | Sodium: 88 mg | Carbs: 29 g | Sugars: 22.3 g

Thin Mint

A mint-chocolate-on-your-pillow kind of treat in smoothie form. This creamy smoothie is high in protein and fiber, thanks mostly to the coconut flour. Coconut flour is an awesome smoothie thickener. It's also low in carbs and gluten-free. And you won't taste a coconut flavor. Soaking the coconut flour in a bit of the milk 10 minutes before blending increases the creamy texture to cloud levels. Want this smoothie less sweet? Use less maple syrup.

MAKES 2 (8-OZ [240-ML]) SMOOTHIES

4 fresh mint leaves

2 tbsp (22 g) chocolate chips

2 tbsp (14 g) coconut flour

2 tbsp (30 ml) maple syrup

⅓ cup (80 ml) yogurt

½ cup (120 ml) milk

½ cup (70 g) ice

Add all the ingredients to a blender and process until the mixture is smooth. Enjoy immediately.

· ·

SUBSTITUTIONS: Substitute the fresh mint with 1 teaspoon of mint extract, replace the yogurt with milk, use 2 dates instead of the maple syrup and use half a banana instead of the coconut flour.

Protein: 3.6 g | Fiber: 1 g | Fat: 4.4 g | Calories: 157 | Sodium: 77 mg | Carbs: 25.3 g | Sugars: 21.7 g

Tropical Kale Soft Serve

Follow a night of revelry with this soothing, veggie-rich smoothie to restore your potassium and boost your fiber intake. The frosty creation looks like a tropical dessert but in fact is full of detox power that will flush your system, restore balance and boost your immunity. The nutritional power comes from every ingredient: fiber and vitamin K from kale, vitamin C from pineapple, potassium from avocado and anti-inflammatories from coconut milk. Still, don't be intimidated by all this nutrition—serve it with a paper umbrella and don your flip-flops.

MAKES 2 (8-OZ [240-ML]) SMOOTHIES

½ cup (33 g) kale leaves

1 cup (164 g) pineapple

1 avocado, pitted and peeled

½ cup (120 ml) coconut milk, canned

1 cup (140 g) ice

Add all the ingredients to a blender and process until the mixture is smooth. Enjoy immediately.

. . . .

SUBSTITUTIONS: Replace the kale with any leafy greens, including spinach, collard greens or romaine. If you don't have pineapple, use mango instead, but the drink will be sweeter.

Protein: 3.4 g | Fiber: 8.1 g | Fat: 29.7 g | Calories: 354 | Sodium: 39 mg | Carbs: 24.2 g | Sugars: 9.6 g

Passion Fruit Frosty

Spinach is the perfect leafy green to match the powerfully fragrant and deliciously sweet passion fruit. The mild green—and I recommend using baby spinach—allows the flavor of passion fruit to shine in a frosty drink so fragrant and hydrating. Together, the pair powers your day with fiber, vitamin C, vitamin A and other nutrients that balance your happy hormones. Raise your spirits higher by adding some goji berries, an Asian berry available worldwide as a dried raisin-like treat, known as the happy berry because of its ability to trigger endorphins. Apart from the nutrition of this smoothie, the fragrant smell alone will transport you to a happier place.

MAKES 2 (8-OZ [240-ML]) SMOOTHIES

½ cup (15 g) spinach leaves

½ cup (120 g) passion fruit pulp

¼ cup (38 g) green grapes

2 tbsp (18 g) goji berries

1 cup (240 ml) ice water

Add all the ingredients to a blender and process until the mixture is smooth. Enjoy immediately.

. . . .

SUBSTITUTIONS: It's not easy to find passion fruit—it is seasonal and you'll find it in quality produce counters. If you can't find the pulp, you can use passion fruit juice instead, although the smoothie will have less fiber. I recommend the brand Ceres. If you want to make this particular recipe without it, replace the passion fruit with more green grapes or peeled kiwi. The goji berries are a mood booster, but not essential here.

Protein: 1.9 g | Fiber: 7.5 g | Fat: 1 g | Calories: 107 | Sodium: 23 mg | Carbs: 24.6 g | Sugars: 16 g

Parsley Power Juice

Parsley Power Juice is the perfect name for this drink because any partakers are certainly being given parsley powers—and those are abundant indeed. This delicious green is top at reducing inflammation, easing muscle pain, cleansing and blocking free radicals, which can lead to disease. Paired with green tea, the detox and immunity powers compound. And we haven't even begun to talk about the benefits of celery and citrus juice. Suffice it to say, you'll want this juice perhaps once a week, especially during flu season. This juice does impart a strong green flavor, but drinking it extra cold helps soften the sharp taste.

MAKES 2 (8-OZ [240-ML]) JUICES

½ cup (30 g) parsley

1 cup (240 ml) green tea

¼ cup (25 g) celery

½ cup (120 ml) lime juice

Add all the ingredients to a blender and process until the mixture is smooth. Pour through a fine sieve and reserve the liquid as your juice. Enjoy right away over ice or refrigerate and drink within 48 hours for optimal nutritional benefit.

NO-WASTE TIP:
The pulp left in the sieve is actually high in nutrition—freeze it and toss it into any smoothie as a boost.

SUBSTITUTIONS: In a pinch, you can replace the parsley with another leafy green, but that is not ideal. The celery is a bonus but not essential to this recipe.

Protein: 0.7 g | Fiber: 1 g | Fat: 0.3 g | Calories: 20 | Sodium: 28 mg | Carbs: 5.4 g | Sugars: 1.1 g

Strawberry-Beet Juice

Strawberry juice with beet greens will soon become your favorite if you like strawberries but don't need an extra sweet flavor in your healthy juices. That's me! I really don't like sweet juices, but I love strawberries. This one turns out even better when you use pre-season strawberries, before they become summer sweet. The beet greens are nutritionally awesome because they actually provide some of the detox and immunity of beets without getting your hands stained. And the thyme lends an herbal flavor that will lead you to say, "What is that familiar flavor?" Elusive yet interesting, this is a memorable juice to help build your immunity.

MAKES 2 (8-OZ [240-ML]) JUICES

½ cup (19 g) beet greens

2 cups (300 g) strawberries

6 sprigs fresh thyme

¾ cup (180 ml) coconut water

Add all the ingredients to a blender and process until the mixture is smooth. Pour through a fine sieve and reserve the liquid as your juice. Enjoy right away or refrigerate and drink within 48 hours for optimal nutritional benefit.

. . . .

NO-WASTE TIP:
The pulp left in the sieve is actually high in nutrition—freeze it and toss it into any smoothie as a boost.

SUBSTITUTIONS: Replace the beet greens with other leafy greens for other benefits. Use blackberries in place of strawberries. The thyme is interesting but not essential.

Protein: 2.8 g | Fiber: 5.9 g | Fat: 0.9 g | Calories: 80 | Sodium: 184 mg | Carbs: 18.1 g | Sugars: 9.7 g

Butter Lettuce-Ginger Juice

Introduce salad to your morning juice. Stuffing green leaves into your blender boosts your juice's levels of antioxidants, those substances that flush toxins from your body, including skin cells, brightening your color. Lettuces in general contain high levels of vitamin C, vitamin A and folic acid, among the three most powerful vitamins for supporting your skin, nails, hair and more. I step out of the box here with butter lettuce, also called Boston or Bibb lettuce, which has among the highest levels of beauty vitamins as well as an easy-to-drink subtle green flavor. Ginger and citrus add a flavorful punch!

MAKES 2 (8-OZ [240-ML]) JUICES

1 cup (54 g) butter lettuce

1 tsp fresh ginger, peeled and minced

1½ cups (278 g) oranges, peeled

¾ cup (105 g) ice

Add all the ingredients to a blender and process until the mixture is smooth. Pour through a fine sieve and reserve the liquid as your juice. Enjoy immediately.

SUBSTITUTIONS: Replace the butter lettuce with any leafy greens of mild flavor such as romaine lettuce or baby leafy greens such as spinach or kale.

Protein: 1.1 g | Fiber: 2.1 g | Fat: 0.2 g | Calories: 56 | Sodium: 3 mg | Carbs: 14.2 g | Sugars: 10.5 g

NO-WASTE TIP:
The pulp left in the sieve is actually high in nutrition—freeze it and toss it into any smoothie as a boost.

Kiwi-Cherry Shot

Low-calorie, sweet kiwi fruit is full of serotonin, a brain chemical that regulates your sleep cycle. Cherries are high in sleep-supporting melatonin. Chamomile tea and poppy seeds provide a heavy downward energy to help you drift off to sleep. All together, a potent sleep potion. Say that three times fast. Or just go to sleep.

MAKES 1 (4-OZ [120-ML]) SHOT

¼ cup (44 g) kiwi

½ cup (120 ml) cherry juice

¼ cup (60 ml) chamomile tea

Pinch of poppy seeds

Add all the ingredients to a blender and process until the mixture is smooth. Pour through a fine sieve, reserving the liquid as your shot. Drink at once or multiply the recipe, pour the shots into ice cube trays and freeze, thawing as you need one.

. . . .

NO-WASTE TIP: The pulp left in the sieve is actually high in nutrition—freeze it and toss it into any smoothie as a boost.

SUBSTITUTIONS: The kiwi and cherry juice cannot be replaced, but you can use water instead of chamomile tea and leave out the poppy seeds.

Protein: 3 g | Fiber: 6.6 g | Fat: 1.3 g | Calories: 172 | Sodium: 8 mg | Carbs: 40.6 g | Sugars: 15 g

Matcha-Mint Shot

Matcha is a super drink, so formulating a concentrated version for a shot makes sense. Matcha is a wonderful brain booster because of the amino acid L-theanine, which simultaneously calms and prods the brain into action, boosting concentration and focus. The mint provides bonus stimulation and flavor. Take this shot before a big day and reap the benefits.

MAKES 1 (4-OZ [120-ML]) SHOT

½ tsp matcha powder

½ cup (120 ml) hot milk

2 fresh mint leaves

Make matcha tea by adding the matcha powder to the milk. Allow it to cool. Add all the ingredients to a blender and process until the mixture is smooth. Pour through a fine sieve, reserving the liquid as your shot. Drink at once or multiply the recipe, pour the shots into ice cube trays and freeze, thawing as you need one.

NO-WASTE TIP:
The pulp left in the sieve is actually high in nutrition—freeze it and toss it into any smoothie as a boost.

SUBSTITUTIONS: The mint is not essential but adds flavor. There is no exact replacement for matcha powder. You can add a green tea bag to the milk instead of the matcha powder, but the shot will be less potent.

Protein: 1 g | Fiber: 1 g | Fat: 1.3 g | Calories: 37 | Sodium: 73 mg | Carbs: 5 g | Sugars: 3 g

Drinking Sunshine:
FRESH FRUIT SMOOTHIES & JUICES

My favorite time to drink a fruit smoothie is the morning. Of course, you can drink them any time of day, but smoothies crafted with fruits provide a useful beginning to the day. That's because they are wonderfully filling, providing fiber and protein to help you feel full until lunch. They are also especially hydrating, which is important in the morning after a night of sleep has left you dehydrated. And many fruit enzymes work with your body processes to energize, boost metabolism that burns fat, clean out your digestive system, enhance your immunity and more.

A few of my favorites in this chapter include my Pomegranate Frosty (page 50), a powerhouse of nutrition your body didn't know it needed; my Coconut-Chocolate Cream (page 63) smoothie to keep you alert through your morning meetings; a Grapefruit-Mint Juice (page 73) to help control your weight; and a powerful Orange-Turmeric Shot (page 77) to boost your immune system. Choose your fruit and you are bound to find a smoothie in this chapter that uses it. Good morning!

Pomegranate Frosty

This fresh, creamy drink sings chords of sweet and sour, thanks to the balance of sweet pomegranate, tangy lime and yogurt. Pomegranates are among the most nutritionally powerful fruits, with compounds that boost energy, help fight disease, reduce joint pain and more. If you can obtain a fresh pomegranate, break it open and scoop out the glowing red jewels called arils, rinse and add those to your smoothie. Bottled pomegranate juice is often easier to obtain year round.

MAKES 2 (8-OZ [240-ML]) SMOOTHIES

½ cup (87 g) pomegranate arils, frozen

½ cup (62 g) raspberries, frozen

2 tbsp (30 ml) lime juice

½ cup (120 ml) yogurt

⅔ cup (94 g) ice

Add all the ingredients to a blender and process until the mixture is smooth. Enjoy immediately, or if you prefer, refrigerate for an hour to give it an extra chill.

· ·

SUBSTITUTIONS: Use ¼ cup (60 ml) of pomegranate juice instead of the arils. Or swap the pomegranates for more raspberries. The fiber will be similar, but the smoothie will be a bit lower in protein, vitamin K and potassium.

Protein: 3.9 g | Fiber: 3.1 g | Fat: 1 g | Calories: 142 | Sodium: 52 mg | Carbs: 30 g | Sugars: 16.1 g

Strawberry-Ginger Cream

A decadent strawberry and cream smoothie with a gingery twist and subtle hint of fresh lime. All these flavors are delivered deliciously in a frosty, creamy drink that can be eaten with a straw or spoon. It's perfect for a sustaining morning meal with 14 grams of protein provided by the yogurt, milk and chia seeds. Potassium is essential for nearly every process in the human body, yet the traditional daily diet of the Western world does not provide nearly enough. Well, this smoothie provides nearly 1,000 ml, about one-quarter of the recommended daily requirement. A smart start to your day!

MAKES 2 (8-OZ [240-ML]) SMOOTHIES

2 cups (300 g) strawberries

2 tbsp (12 g) ginger, peeled and crushed

2 tbsp (20 g) chia seeds

½ cup (120 ml) lime juice

½ cup (120 ml) yogurt

¼ cup (60 ml) milk

¼ cup (35 g) ice

Add all the ingredients to a blender and process until the mixture is smooth. Enjoy immediately.

. . . .

SUBSTITUTIONS: Use 1 tablespoon (6 g) of ground ginger if you can't find fresh ginger. Leaving out the chia seeds won't change the flavor but it will reduce the protein.

Protein: 9.4 g | Fiber: 12.9 g | Fat: 10.3 g | Calories: 248 | Sodium: 76 mg | Carbs: 32.4 g | Sugars: 13 g

Apple Rolled Oats

Fall: raking leaves, drinking cider. All these comforting memories come swirling in on the first sip of this energizing smoothie. I love how easy the ingredients are to find for this smoothie. Any apple is welcome here: Gala, green, golden, even old and bruised. If you choose a more sour apple, just taste-test and add another date for more sweetness. Want a less-sweet smoothie? Don't add the dates. Let your apple provide the sweetness. And did someone say energy? Apples are packed with vitamins, minerals and fiber, and so are rolled oats. This smoothie will chug along slowly through your system for hours, providing you with boundless energy all the way.

MAKES 2 (8-OZ [240-ML]) SMOOTHIES

2 cups (240 g) apples, not peeled

1 cup (90 g) rolled oats

2 dates, soaked and pitted

1 tsp ground apple pie spice

¼ cup (60 ml) milk

¼ cup (35 g) ice

Add all the ingredients to a blender and process until the mixture is smooth. Enjoy immediately.

. . . .

SUBSTITUTIONS: You can use quick oats instead of rolled oats, but try to find some that are unsweetened and have few additives. No dates? Two tablespoons (30 ml) of maple syrup can replace the 2 dates.

Protein: 6.3 g | Fiber: 10.2 g | Fat: 3.4 g | Calories: 302 | Sodium: 22 mg | Carbs: 65.7 g | Sugars: 29.6 g

Chocolate Orange

Orange has long been touted for its talent for bringing out chocolate's depth of flavor. This is especially true when you use quality chocolate, as in cacao powder. Cacao powder is made from a dried cocoa bean, just like the more mainstream unsweetened cocoa powder you are probably more used to seeing. However, unlike cocoa powder, cacao powder is minimally processed, so it retains more natural nutrition. And nutritionally robust it is! Cacao powder has many nutritional benefits, but here I'll note its mood-boosting power. It has several compounds that work to raise your feelings of well-being including one that pumps dopamine into your system, helping you feel happy and content. So make this smoothie and sip yourself to a happier place.

MAKES 2 (8-OZ [240-ML]) SMOOTHIES

3 tbsp (16 g) cacao powder

1½ cups (278 g) oranges, peeled

½ zucchini, raw and not peeled

1 tsp ground cinnamon

¾ cup (180 ml) milk

¾ cup (105 g) ice

Add all the ingredients to a blender and process until the mixture is smooth. Enjoy immediately or refrigerate for later.

. . . .

SUBSTITUTIONS: Instead of cacao powder, use unsweetened cocoa powder or ¼ cup (44 g) of quality chocolate chips with at least 70 percent cacao. Microwave the chips at 15-second intervals until they melt, then blend the melted chocolate into the smoothie.

Protein: 3.7 g | Fiber: 4.9 g | Fat: 3 g | Calories: 123 | Sodium: 113 mg | Carbs: 25.3 g | Sugars: 15.7 g

Lavender Lemonade

My Lavender Lemonade recipe was created for a family lemonade stand we run every summer on the sunny lavender-lined sidewalks of Martha's Vineyard. This delicious, frosty drink is tart, lemony and heavily scented with the fresh lavender that prevails on the New England island all summer. I used sparkling water in my recipe to add some fizz and spray to the experience. The aromatherapy effects of the lavender are strong, but ingesting lavender as well is said to have a strong relaxing effect. So take a deep breath, sip and enjoy!

MAKES 2 (8-OZ [240-ML]) SMOOTHIES

1 cup (240 ml) lemon juice

2 tsp (2 g) lavender, culinary buds

2 tbsp (30 ml) maple syrup

1 cup (240 ml) sparkling water

¾ cup (105 g) ice

Add all the ingredients to a blender and process until the mixture is smooth. Drink immediately to enjoy the carbonation, which will dissipate over time.

. . . .

SUBSTITUTIONS: Instead of culinary lavender buds, use 1 teaspoon of lavender extract. Want it sweeter? Add more maple syrup, but be sure to add a teaspoon at a time and taste-test.

Protein: 1 g | Fiber: 0.5 g | Fat: 1 g | Calories: 81 | Sodium: 26 mg | Carbs: 16 g | Sugars: 14.5 g

Orange Creamsicle

Who hasn't been told to eat an orange when they have a cold? Well, it's great advice! Oranges are full of vitamin C, a strong antioxidant known to battle disease and protect our organs. But the body cannot produce vitamin C, so consuming it is important. This smoothie alone provides 300 milligrams of the vitamin, which is about 400 percent of the recommended daily allowance set by the U.S. Food and Drug Administration. Eating oranges straight is fun, but this smoothie whips them into a creamy vanilla treat straight out of an old-fashioned ice cream shop. If you are going to fight a cold, you might as well have a little celebration, right?

MAKES 2 (8-OZ [240-ML]) SMOOTHIES

1½ cups (278 g) orange slices, without peel

1 tbsp (6 g) orange peel, chopped

½ cup (120 ml) milk

½ cup (70 g) ice

1 tsp vanilla extract

Pinch of ground cinnamon

Add all the ingredients to a blender and process until the mixture is smooth. Enjoy immediately or refrigerate for later.

SUBSTITUTIONS: The orange slices and peel can be swapped for 1 cup (240 ml) of not-from-concentrate orange juice. If you make this swap, use yogurt instead of milk to thicken the smoothie.

Protein: 1.8 g | Fiber: 3.3 g | Fat: 0.6 g | Calories: 103 | Sodium: 38 mg | Carbs: 24 g | Sugars: 18.5 g

Blueberry Date

A delicious, purple berry shake sweetened with dates. Dates are high in fiber, potassium and manganese and have a delicious caramel sweetness, so no sugar is needed. Dates are also the perfect complement to blueberries, which are not very sweet and also high in fiber. Just one Blueberry Date smoothie contains nearly 5 grams of fiber, one-fifth of the daily recommendation by the American Heart Association! Add in protein-rich yogurt and ground flaxseed, and you have a berry-licious smoothie that will keep you feeling full and satisfied.

MAKES 2 (8-OZ [240-ML]) SMOOTHIES

1 cup (148 g) blueberries

2 dates, soaked and pitted

2 tbsp (14 g) ground flaxseed

½ tsp ground cinnamon

¾ cup (180 ml) plain yogurt

¼ cup (60 ml) milk

¼ cup (35 g) ice

Add all the ingredients to a blender and process until the mixture is smooth. Enjoy immediately, or if you prefer, refrigerate for later.

· ·

SUBSTITUTIONS: Any berry you have on hand would make a fine substitute for blueberries within this date shake.

Protein: 7.3 g | Fiber: 4.6 g | Fat: 3.6 g | Calories: 169 | Sodium: 67 mg | Carbs: 25.7 g | Sugars: 19 g

Coconut-Chocolate Cream

The coconut, the brown hairy fruit off a coconut palm tree—has three botanical classifications: nut, seed and fruit, with botanists putting the emphasis on fruit. I love this tasty fruit because both its meat and milk offer a wealth of protein and a panel of essential amino acids that support many of our body's processes. Coconut milk, especially the canned variety, can turn any smoothie into a decadent yet healthy beverage. Be sure to use unsweetened, canned coconut milk, not the refrigerated version, which has added sugars. Here I mixed the coconut milk with almond milk to keep the protein up and the fat down, although coconut fats are healthier than other dietary fats; they encourage fat burning and raise good cholesterol. The resulting smoothie is a protein-rich chocolate meal posing as a decadent milkshake.

MAKES 2 (8-OZ [240-ML]) SMOOTHIES

½ cup (120 ml) coconut milk, canned

¾ cup (180 ml) almond milk

3 tbsp (16 g) cacao powder

2 tbsp (30 ml) maple syrup

1 tsp vanilla extract

Pinch of ground cinnamon

Add all the ingredients to a blender and process until the mixture is smooth. Enjoy immediately, or if you prefer, refrigerate for an hour to give it an extra chill.

. . . .

SUBSTITUTIONS: You can adjust the ratio of the two milks depending on what you have on hand. Replacing some of the coconut milk with regular milk will lower the fat but also make the smoothie thinner in texture. Unsweetened cocoa powder can be used instead of cacao powder.

Protein: 3.8 g | Fiber: 2.4 g | Fat: 22 g | Calories: 323 | Sodium: 118 mg | Carbs: 28.9 g | Sugars: 18.3 g

Berry Earl Grey

A healthy fruit smoothie spin on the popular black tea drink, the London Fog, this brain booster will wake you up gently, with no caffeinated crash. Earl Grey tea is a black tea that contains caffeine but also L-theanine, a relaxer amino acid, so while it prods you awake, it asks you to remain calm. Add in fiber-rich berries, and you have a morning drink that will not only wake you but also help you feel full until lunch. The berries—my preference is blueberries, raspberries and strawberries—make a healthier sweetener than the syrup normally associated with a London Fog. And they contribute their own antioxidants. So, while I like to call this smoothie a brain-booster, it could also go under the immunity category as well. Or a "tastes great" category.

MAKES 2 (8-OZ [240-ML]) SMOOTHIES

⅔ cup (160 ml) water

2 Earl Grey tea bags

⅓ cup (80 ml) almond milk

1½ cups (220 g) mixed berries, frozen

½ tsp vanilla extract, optional

Make the Earl Grey tea by heating the water and allowing both tea bags to steep in it for 10 minutes. Then, add the almond milk and allow the tea to cool.

Once the tea is cool, add the tea, berries and vanilla, if using, to a blender and process until the mixture is smooth. Serve over ice.

SUBSTITUTIONS: Teas that taste similar and have a similar energizing function to Earl Grey include rooibos tea and matcha. And any mix of berries you have on hand is fine. The vanilla is optional, but represents the vanilla syrup used in the London Fog.

Protein: 1 g | Fiber: 2.6 g | Fat: 0.8 g | Calories: 75 | Sodium: 24 mg | Carbs: 17.2 g | Sugars: 11.9 g

Strawberry Kiwi

This pretty pink and green smoothie is a wonderful snack to eat around one hour before bed to achieve a healthier, deeper sleep. That's because the kiwi fruit is extremely high in serotonin, a substance that the body needs to initiate and sustain a healthy sleep. I've always thought kiwis look like a fuzzy mini-melon. They're a bit of work to peel, but worth it for a good night's sleep. I paired them here with strawberries to give the smoothie more flavor since kiwis taste rather neutral. Zucchini is in there to thicken the drink, and a date is added to sweeten and provide sleep-sustaining fiber. Good night, sweet dreams.

MAKES 2 (8-OZ [240-ML]) SMOOTHIES

1 cup (150 g) strawberries

½ cup (88 g) kiwi, peeled

¼ cup (28 g) zucchini, raw and not peeled

1 date, soaked and pitted

½ cup (120 ml) milk

½ cup (70 g) ice

1 tsp ground cinnamon

Add all the ingredients to a blender and process until the mixture is smooth. Enjoy immediately or refrigerate for the next day.

. . . .

SUBSTITUTIONS: You can use blueberries or even a banana if you don't have strawberries. I wouldn't replace the kiwi if you are after sleep support. And the date is not essential here but provides sweetness as well as more fiber and nutrients.

Protein: 1 g | Fiber: 1.8 g | Fat: 0.9 g | Calories: 56 | Sodium: 38 mg | Carbs: 12.1 g | Sugars: 8.4 g

Pear-Hibiscus Tea

I love making recipes with hibiscus tea in part because of its glorious color: a deep, vibrant pink! But I also love it as an ingredient for my smoothies because of the powerful nutritional benefits this tea provides. When brewed into a tea and consumed, the flavorful flower is considered effective in blocking free radicals, those unstable molecules that can cause cell damage in your body, especially to your skin. So this smoothie is wonderful at protecting skin from the signs of aging. But what I love best about hibiscus tea is its unique flavor—kind of tangy, like citrus-crossed cranberries. Sweetening this smoothie with pear and lime creates the perfect fresh balance. To make it extra fancy, you can coat the rim of your glass with coconut oil, and press it into a dish of crushed freeze-dried berries.

MAKES 2 (8-OZ [240-ML]) SMOOTHIES

1½ cups (360 ml) water

2 hibiscus tea bags

1 pear, cored and chopped

¼ cup (60 ml) lime juice

1 cup (240 ml) ice water

Boil the water, add the hibiscus tea bags and allow the tea to steep for 20 minutes or long enough to cool. Discard the tea bags and add the tea to a blender. Then add the pear, lime juice and ice water. Process briefly until the drink is just combined. Serve this beautiful pink drink over ice.

SUBSTITUTIONS: If you want the beauty support and don't have hibiscus tea, try chamomile or green tea. Both are known to be rich in similar free radical–fighting antioxidants. To make the smoothie sweeter, add more pear.

Protein: 0.3 g | Fiber: 2.2 g | Fat: 0.1 g | Calories: 43 | Sodium: 1 mg | Carbs: 11.5 g | Sugars: 7 g

Cranberry Orange

Your skin will thank you for drinking this smoothie. Cranberries provide awesome support for collagen production within our body. And collagen on the inside translates to glowing skin on the outside. Cranberries also have anti-aging powers, so they're a perfect tool to reduce wrinkles. Here, combining it with vitamin C–rich oranges is wise since vitamin C is also beneficial to healthy skin. I added mushrooms as a thickener to this smoothie since they are full of vitamin D, selenium and other properties that protect skin. Nope, you can't taste the mushrooms.

MAKES 2 (8-OZ [240-ML]) SMOOTHIES

1 cup (100 g) cranberries, frozen

1½ cups (278 g) orange slices, without peel

6 mushrooms, fresh

2 tsp (10 ml) lemon juice

¾ cup (180 ml) ice water

Add all the ingredients to a blender and process until the mixture is smooth. Enjoy immediately.

. . . .

SUBSTITUTIONS: If you can't find fresh or frozen cranberries, don't use the canned version you'd use for Thanksgiving. Instead, substitute blackberries or even pomegranate arils. I use white button mushrooms here, and it's what I recommend for their neutral flavor.

Protein: 3 g | Fiber: 5.8 g | Fat: 0.4 g | Calories: 106 | Sodium: 4 mg | Carbs: 22.7 g | Sugars: 15.7 g

Peach Soft Serve

Every time I eat this smoothie, I imagine myself on a treadmill—even though I don't own one. And that's because I know that peaches are incredible at boosting metabolism. They have these elements called flavonoids that prod your metabolism into running like the wind. And a racing metabolism is an awesome way to burn calories and control weight. Plus, it tastes like a peach version of Disney's DOLE Whip®, only far healthier.

MAKES 2 (8-OZ [240-ML]) SMOOTHIES

1 cup (154 g) peach slices, fresh

½ cup (82 g) mango chunks, frozen

¼ cup (60 g) garbanzo beans, canned, drained and rinsed

½ cup (120 ml) milk

½ cup (70 g) ice

Add all the ingredients to a blender and process until the mixture is smooth yet frosty. Enjoy immediately.

. . . .

SUBSTITUTIONS: If you can't find fresh or frozen peaches, double the amount of mango. Mangoes aren't as effective in boosting metabolism as peaches are, but they are packed with fiber, which will make you feel full and thus eat less, also useful in supporting weight control.

Protein: 9.9 g | Fiber: 6.2 g | Fat: 1.9 g | Calories: 185 | Sodium: 69 mg | Carbs: 34.8 g | Sugars: 21.3 g

Cantaloupe Frosty

Cantaloupe makes for a wonderfully creamy smoothie. And it is a robust mood booster because it is packed with beta-carotene, a powerful antioxidant that is associated with lifting spirits and dampening depression. You can identify foods that have loads of beta-carotene by color: think carrots, pumpkin, peaches and sweet potatoes. I combined the melon with raspberries to add fiber and yogurt for the protein. The result is a luscious smoothie that can be served as a beverage or as soft serve in a bowl.

MAKES 2 (8-OZ [240-ML]) SMOOTHIES

1 cup (156 g) cantaloupe, frozen

1 cup (123 g) raspberries, frozen

1 cup (240 ml) yogurt

¼ cup (60 ml) milk

¼ cup (35 g) ice

Add all the ingredients to a blender and process until the mixture is smooth. Enjoy immediately.

SUBSTITUTIONS: If you cannot find fresh cantaloupe, fresh or frozen peaches would be the perfect substitute. Raspberries cannot really be substituted and result in the same color and texture.

Protein: 8.4 g | Fiber: 4.7 g | Fat: 2.1 g | Calories: 146 | Sodium: 99 mg | Carbs: 22.3 g | Sugars: 17.5 g

Grapefruit-Mint Juice

Grapefruit has long been used as a means toward weight loss. Even as far back as the 1930s, people were embarking on a grapefruit diet to lose weight. Since then, science has shown that grapefruit contains an antioxidant, called naringenin, that helps burn fat faster. Aloe vera, the juice from the aloe vera plant, boosts metabolism, also supporting fat loss. This combo in a juice is quite easy to make and delicious to drink. Adding mint tempers the sourness of the grapefruit and brightens the overall flavor. A fun drink to add to any weight-control regime.

MAKES 2 (8-OZ [240-ML]) JUICES

1 cup (230 g) grapefruit segments, fresh

2 tbsp (30 ml) aloe vera juice

2 tbsp (11 g) fresh mint

½ cup (120 ml) water

Add all the ingredients to a blender and process until the mixture is smooth. Pour through a fine sieve and reserve the liquid as your juice. Enjoy right away or refrigerate and drink within 48 hours for optimum nutritional benefit.

NO-WASTE TIP:
The pulp left in the sieve is actually high in nutrition—freeze it and toss it into any smoothie as a boost.

SUBSTITUTIONS: The grapefruit is essential, but you can replace the aloe vera with blueberries, which also speed up metabolism. The mint leaves add a potent fresh flavor, but half a teaspoon of mint extract would work as well.

Protein: 0.9 g | Fiber: 1.7 g | Fat: 0.2 g | Calories: 43 | Sodium: 14 mg | Carbs: 10.8 g | Sugars: 8 g

Strawberry-Basil Juice

Strawberries are full of antioxidants and vitamin C, making them powerful immune system boosters. Paired with basil leaves, which are full of anti-inflammatory and anti-bacterial components, this juice is a super immunity booster. And lemon—both fruit and peel—have copious amounts of vitamin C. Plus the citrus pairs well with the sweet strawberry flavor. I often reach for a sharp-tasting spicy juice when I feel a cold coming on, so it was a splendid surprise to realize this mild-flavored juice with the fruity herbal fragrance is equally up to the task of chasing away that beginning niggle of a sore throat.

MAKES 2 (8-OZ [240-ML]) JUICES

½ cup (50 g) cauliflower florets

½ cup (75 g) strawberries

¼ cup (6 g) fresh basil

½ lemon, including peel, chopped

1 cup (240 ml) ice water

For the creamiest result, first steam and cool your cauliflower. Then, add all the ingredients to a blender and process until the mixture is smooth. Pour through a fine sieve and reserve the liquid as your juice. Enjoy right away or refrigerate and drink within 48 hours for optimal nutritional benefit.

*See photo on page 8.

NO-WASTE TIP:
The pulp left in the sieve is actually high in nutrition—freeze it and toss it into any smoothie as a boost.

SUBSTITUTIONS: The strawberries can be swapped out for other vitamin C-rich berries, such as blueberries, raspberries and even blackberries, but the flavor won't be the same. The cauliflower can be omitted, and if basil can't be used, try fresh mint.

Protein: 1 g | Fiber: 1.8 g | Fat: 0.2 g | Calories: 23 | Sodium: 8 mg | Carbs: 5.5 g | Sugars: 2.7 g

Chocolate-Raspberry Shot

A chocolate-raspberry shot? Why not? Chocolate has enormous health benefits, as well as a wonderful energizing ability. Raspberries are full of antioxidants. Add energizing hot chili powder and you will be skipping your way down the hallways at work. Ok, well, maybe skipping isn't your thing, but you will have enough energy to do so. And your energy spike will not crash. That's because the substance in chocolate that acts as caffeine is theobromine, which is dispersed more slowly through your system and doesn't produce the spike and crash that comes from caffeinated coffee. Happy skipping!

MAKES 1 (4-OZ [120-ML]) SHOT

4 raspberries

1 tbsp (5 g) cacao powder

1 tsp maple syrup

½ tsp ground chili powder

½ cup (120 ml) almond milk

Add all the ingredients to a blender and process until the mixture is smooth. Pour through a fine sieve, reserving the liquid as your shot. Drink at once or multiply the recipe, pour the shots into ice cube trays and freeze, thawing as you need one.

· ·

SUBSTITUTIONS: Use cayenne pepper instead of chili powder. Any berry can be used in place of raspberries. Unsweetened cocoa powder can be used instead of cacao powder.

Protein: 5.6 g | Fiber: 11.4 g | Fat: 6 g | Calories: 141 | Sodium: 85 mg | Carbs: 28.3 g | Sugars: 10.4 g

NO-WASTE TIP:
The pulp left in the sieve is actually high in nutrition—freeze it and toss it into any smoothie as a boost.

Orange-Turmeric Shot

A golden shot in so many ways. Gold in color thanks to the curcumin found in turmeric. Curcumin is a pigment in the spice that actually works to reduce inflammation in the body, thus keeping the immune system working efficiently. Oranges add their own gold, in the form of high levels of vitamin C. The black pepper and coconut oil are important players to help you better absorb the turmeric's magical powers. I make immunity shots like this every other day during flu season. They are a powerful weapon when you need your immune system amped up.

MAKES 1 (4-OZ [120-ML]) SHOT

⅓ cup (62 g) oranges, peeled

¼ cup (60 ml) coconut water

½ tsp coconut oil

1 tsp ground turmeric

Pinch of black pepper

Add all the ingredients to a blender and process until the mixture is smooth. Pour through a fine sieve, reserving the liquid as your shot. Drink at once or multiply the recipe, pour the shots into ice cube trays and freeze, thawing as you need one.

. . . .

SUBSTITUTIONS: Other citrus can replace the oranges and water can replace the coconut water. The coconut meat or even coconut flour can be used instead of coconut oil. Cayenne pepper can be used instead of black pepper. There are no substitutions for the turmeric.

Protein: 1.2 g | Fiber: 2.6 g | Fat: 2.7 g | Calories: 67 | Sodium: 64 mg | Carbs: 10.7 g | Sugars: 7.3 g

NO-WASTE TIP:
The pulp left in the sieve is actually high in nutrition—freeze it and toss it into any smoothie as a boost.

Red Grapes-Tomato ACV Shot

This shot is exploding with protective phytochemicals. Think of phytochemicals as tiny soldiers marching into battle to protect you from disease and aging. One such soldier, resveratrol, protects against many diseases and is found in red grapes. Tomatoes are filled with the protective antioxidant lycopene. Finally, the apple cider vinegar (ACV) is cleansing and converts your body pH to a healthier base state, which is a better environment for you to stay well. Don your armor.

MAKES 1 (4-OZ [120-ML]) SHOT

⅓ cup (50 g) red grapes

3 cherry tomatoes

2 tbsp (30 ml) apple cider vinegar

⅓ cup (80 ml) water

Add all the ingredients to a blender and process until the mixture is smooth. Pour through a fine sieve, reserving the liquid as your shot. Drink at once or multiply the recipe, pour the shots into ice cube trays and freeze, thawing as you need one.

NO-WASTE TIP:
The pulp left in the sieve is actually high in nutrition—freeze it and toss it into any smoothie as a boost.

SUBSTITUTIONS: Tomatoes contain the most significant amount of lycopene of any food, so there is no suitable replacement for them. Blueberries and cranberries can replace red grapes and provide resveratrol protection. Apple cider vinegar has no replacement. Be sure to use a quality ACV; I recommend Bragg brand. You need a version that includes the "mother," the sediment that carries the necessary nutrients to make the ACV effective.

Protein: 0.7 g | Fiber: 1 g | Fat: 0.2 g | Calories: 38 | Sodium: 5 mg | Carbs: 8 g | Sugars: 6.7 g

Glowing Glass:
SUPERFOOD SMOOTHIES & JUICES

In my view, there are two types of superfoods. There are those mainstream foods that are so potently nutritious that they deserve superfood status. And there are those obscure products, a root here, a berry there, that may have a unique nutritional power, but typically only achieve scattered and spotty attention. In this chapter, I provide smoothies that use a bit of both types.

The mainstream superfoods in this chapter celebrate ingredients such as nuts, berries, beans, veggies, pseudo grains, seeds and chocolate. For instance, I think you'll love my Chocolate Chia pudding (page 94). This dessert is so decadent, you'd never guess it's also a potent source of protein and fiber. And then there is my Coconut Cream Spice (page 86) made velvety with white beans. And if you've never bought buckwheat groats, I challenge you to make my creamy Buckwheat Overnight Oats (page 99).

In this chapter, I also share smoothies using the more obscure superfoods, including baobab, açai, dragon fruit, goji berries and spirulina. You'll find spirulina in several recipes in this chapter, both blue and green, since the protein-rich algae powder is a favorite of mine. I even used it in a blue protein shot. Goji berries, the happy berry, is found in my Goji Berries Booster (page 106). And the beautiful pink hues of my Dragon Fruit Dream smoothie (page 89) will be fixed in your mind's eye.

And then there are a few foods I want you to experience that aren't normally found in smoothies but qualify as superfoods because of the concentration of nutrients and flavor they provide.

One is miso, a fermented, umami food that is high in protein and essential nutrients and is often found in Asian savory dishes, but featured here in a salty Miso Hot Chocolate smoothie (page 93). Two others are made with ingredients you'll find familiar but may be surprised to experience in a smoothie. The first, Vanilla Almond Joy (page 102), features chilled white potatoes as a weight reduction tool. The other, my Hummus Fudge Shake (page 105), is created largely with—you guessed it—hummus, or rather the garbanzo beans and tahini used to make hummus.

Smoothies are the perfect way to achieve a more complete nutritional day without doing a lot of cooking, shopping and eating. So it makes sense that we step out of the box regarding what we put in them. Agreed?

Açai Cherry

Cherries are a seasonal fixture in the United States. And being rich in melatonin, they are well-known as the best fruit to eat to support sleep. So are açai berries. This Amazon rainforest fruit is high in amino acids and vitamin B, which together work to help the body's brain and muscles shut down for the night. Find frozen açai pulp in your grocery store, or look for a powdered version—I recommend the brands Terrasoul Superfoods or Navitas® Organics. Add in chia seeds, often sourced from Australia, and your smoothie is filling and able to ward off sleep-interrupting hunger pangs. An international sleep-support smoothie.

MAKES 2 (8-OZ [240-ML]) SMOOTHIES

2 tbsp (20 g) chia seeds

1 cup (240 ml) water

1 (3½-oz [100-g]) açai berry frozen pack or 1 tbsp (6 g) of açai powder

½ cup (69 g) cherries, pitted

¼ cup (44 g) chocolate chips, plus more to top, if desired

Whipped cream, for topping, optional

Add the chia seeds to the water and set aside for 10 minutes to create a pulp. When ready, add the soaked chia seeds and water to a blender. Follow with all the other ingredients. Blend the mixture until it is smooth. Drink or refrigerate in a sealed bottle. When you are ready to drink, stir the mixture if the layers have separated.

. . . .

SUBSTITUTIONS: Replace açai with dragon fruit, mentioned in the Dragon Fruit Dream (page 89). Raspberries can replace cherries in terms of color and texture, but with less sleep-supporting results. In that event, replace some of the water with chamomile tea to increase sleep support.

Protein: 6.8 g | Fiber: 11.2 g | Fat: 15.8 g | Calories: 282 | Sodium: 24 mg | Carbs: 30.4 g | Sugars: 15.6 g

Chocolate Hemp

This chocolate hemp smoothie can not only boost your energy, but also help clear your skin and even balance off-kilter hormones. The energy boost comes primarily from the chocolate, which has caffeine and essential nutrients that fight fatigue. The other benefits come from a tiny white seed called a hemp seed or hemp heart. Rich in healthy fats, protein and a slew of essential minerals, they also contain the amino acid arginine, which has an incredible ability to help lower blood pressure. Sprinkle these magical seeds on your cereal, on your yogurt, on your ice cream or in this rich, milkshake-esque smoothie.

MAKES 2 (8-OZ [240-ML]) SMOOTHIES

⅓ cup (53 g) hemp seeds

2 tbsp (11 g) cacao powder

3 dates, soaked and pitted

1½ cups (360 ml) milk

Pinch of salt

Add all the ingredients to a blender and process until the mixture is smooth. Enjoy immediately, or if you prefer, refrigerate for an hour to give it an extra chill.

• •

SUBSTITUTIONS: No dates? Three tablespoons (45 ml) of maple syrup can replace the 3 dates. Unsweetened cocoa powder can be used instead of cacao powder, however, cacao powder is higher in fiber and magnesium. For quality cacao powder, look for brands like Navitas® Organics, Terrasoul Superfoods, Sunfood™ and Anthony's Goods.

Protein: 9.6 g | Fiber: 3.4 g | Fat: 12.9 g | Calories: 218 | Sodium: 106 mg | Carbs: 19.8 g | Sugars: 12.5 g

Coconut Cream Spice

White beans together with coconut milk create a nutritional firestorm, powering you through your day with nearly 10 grams of protein, as well as fiber and a slew of essential nutrients. You might expect to see white beans in a spicy chili, but they work in a daily smoothie too. I buy canned, organic white beans when possible, rinsing them before blending. They really don't influence the flavor much, but are especially hidden in this smoothie behind the strong spices of cinnamon, cardamom and cloves. A delicious, cold protein smoothie with a flavor that hints at a traditional eggnog.

MAKES 2 (8-OZ [240-ML]) SMOOTHIES

1 cup (240 ml) coconut milk, canned

2 dates, soaked and pitted

¼ cup (65 g) white beans, canned, rinsed and drained

1 tsp ground cinnamon

Pinch of ground cardamom

Pinch of ground cloves

Add all the ingredients to a blender and process until the mixture is smooth. Enjoy immediately, or if you prefer, refrigerate for an hour to give it an extra chill.

• •

SUBSTITUTIONS: The white beans I used were navy beans, but cannellini or white kidney beans work as well. Or you can use black beans, which will change the color a bit. You can use a different milk, but you won't achieve the same thick, creamy texture. Two tablespoons (30 ml) of maple syrup can replace the 2 dates.

Protein: 9.6 g | Fiber: 5.1 g | Fat: 30.3 g | Calories: 455 | Sodium: 97 mg | Carbs: 34.4 g | Sugars: 11.8 g

Dragon Fruit Dream

Get your camera ready—this smoothie is so beautiful, you'll want a photo before you drink. But it's not just another pretty smoothie. Built largely on tropical fruits, this drink has a powerful ability to strengthen your immune system. Dragon fruit, a futuristic-looking pink melon, protects your white blood cells with compounds found in its fruit. Find frozen dragon fruit in your grocery store, or look for a powdered version. I recommend the brands Terrasoul Superfoods, Navitas® Organics and Sunfood™. Mango, another tropical superstar, provides a bright silky flavor, fiber and vitamin C. Throw in raw beets for more pink color, as well as vitamins C and B, potassium and iron—all essential to a strong immune system.

MAKES 2 (8-OZ [240-ML]) SMOOTHIES

1 (3½-oz [100-g]) dragon fruit frozen pack or 1 tbsp (2 g) dragon fruit powder

¼ cup (34 g) beets, raw, peeled and chopped

¾ cup (123 g) frozen mango chunks

½ cup (120 ml) coconut water

Add all the ingredients to a blender and process until the mixture is smooth. Enjoy immediately, or if you prefer, refrigerate for an hour to give it an extra chill.

. . . .

SUBSTITUTIONS: There is no direct replacement for dragon fruit in terms of color, but kiwi stands in nicely regarding flavor. The beets can't be replaced, but a banana can be used instead of mango, although the flavor will be sweeter and less bright.

Protein: 2.7 g | Fiber: 4.2 g | Fat: 1.2 g | Calories: 155 | Sodium: 84 mg | Carbs: 27.9 g | Sugars: 18.6 g

Spirulina Mango

Spirulina—a blue-green algae—is a popular superfood extremely high in a wide range of nutrients. So high in fact, that NASA is exploring growing it in space to feed astronauts. I think the astronauts would consider the flavor of my protein smoothie to be out of this world. It's thick and fruity with mango and even has a hidden vegetable: cauliflower. The color is the same as a beautiful ocean— the result of mixing blue spirulina with orange mango.

MAKES 2 (8-OZ [240-ML]) SMOOTHIES

¼ cup (25 g) cauliflower florets

1 cup (164 g) mango chunks

1 cup (240 ml) milk

1 tsp blue spirulina

For the creamiest result, first steam and cool your cauliflower. Then, add all the ingredients to a blender and process until the mixture is smooth. Enjoy immediately, or if you prefer, refrigerate for an hour to give it an extra chill.

SUBSTITUTIONS: Blue spirulina plays nicely with any strong-flavored fruit—swap out the mango for pineapple or papaya. The cauliflower is a vegetable thickener, but raw, unpeeled zucchini would work as well. So would tofu or yogurt.

Protein: 6.9 g | Fiber: 1.8 g | Fat: 3.1 g | Calories: 124 | Sodium: 99 mg | Carbs: 19.9 g | Sugars: 17.2 g

Miso Hot Chocolate

Raw miso, a salty, fermented paste, adds a hint of a savory flavor to this rich chocolate shake. It's found in the refrigerated areas of grocery stores and is a popular addition to Asian dishes. Miso contributes to the most recently added fifth taste in the culinary world: sweet, bitter, salty, sour and now, umami. Apart from its unusual flavor, miso provides beneficial bacteria to the gut setting up a body environment that boosts immunity. Miso is also high in protein and essential nutrients, including vitamin B6, which supports regulation of moods. Cacao powder has the ability to stimulate the production of endorphins, the happy hormones. But salty chocolate always makes me happy too, so there is a double dose of happy in this glass.

MAKES 2 (8-OZ [240-ML]) SMOOTHIES

2 tsp (12 g) miso

1½ cups (360 ml) milk

3 tbsp (16 g) cacao powder

1 tbsp (15 ml) maple syrup

1 tbsp (15 ml) brewed coffee

1 tsp vanilla extract

Add all the ingredients to a blender and process until the mixture is smooth. Serve hot as cocoa or chill as a smoothie.

• •

SUBSTITUTIONS: There is no substitution for miso. The cacao and maple syrup can be replaced with ¼ cup (44 g) of chocolate chips, melted in the microwave in 30-second intervals. Or unsweetened cocoa powder can be used instead of cacao powder. However, cacao powder is higher in fiber and magnesium. For quality cacao powder, look for brands like Navitas® Organics, Terrasoul Superfoods, Sunfood™ and Anthony's Goods.

Protein: 2.9 g | Fiber: 2.7 g | Fat: 3.3 g | Calories: 101 | Sodium: 321 mg | Carbs: 18.7 g | Sugars: 11 g

Chocolate Chia

Chia seeds have been having a moment for years now, and rightly so. The tiny seeds, popping with protein, fiber, calcium, magnesium and more, are being tossed in cereal and on yogurt everywhere. My favorite way to use them is in smoothies as thickeners and to add fiber and protein. But one interesting aspect of chia seeds is that they swell in liquid, so adding them to chocolate, milk and maple syrup creates a kind of delicious pudding. Customize this recipe by adding more flavors like cinnamon, coffee or mint, or sprinkle with crushed nuts or cacao nibs to enjoy a chocolate creamy treat with nearly 15 grams of fiber per cup.

MAKES 2 (8-OZ [240-ML]) SMOOTHIES

4 tbsp (40 g) chia seeds

1 cup (240 ml) milk

3 tbsp (16 g) cacao powder

3 tbsp (45 ml) maple syrup

½ tsp vanilla extract

Pinch of salt

Add the chia seeds to the milk and set aside for 20 minutes to gel. Add the mixture to a blender, along with all the other ingredients, and process until the mixture is smooth. Drink or spoon the mixture right away, or refrigerate overnight to create a thick pudding.

• •

SUBSTITUTIONS: Unsweetened cocoa powder can be used instead of cacao powder.

Protein: 8 g | Fiber: 14.4 g | Fat: 11.4 g | Calories: 266 | Sodium: 74 mg | Carbs: 42.6 g | Sugars: 21 g

Tofu-Berry Protein

Tofu is an excellent smoothie thickener and provides tons of protein but few calories. Using a silken variety would give you the creamiest texture, but any texture will work provided you adjust the milk. The tofu has a neutral flavor, so the apple and blueberry flavors take center stage. This drink is a stunning purplish blue, depending on the color intensity of your blueberries.

MAKES 2 (8-OZ [240-ML]) SMOOTHIES

1 cup (148 g) blueberries

½ cup (60 g) apples, not peeled

¼ cup (62 g) tofu

½ cup (120 ml) almond milk

Pinch of ground cinnamon

Add all the ingredients to a blender and process until the mixture is smooth. Enjoy immediately, or if you prefer, refrigerate for an hour to give it an extra chill.

. . . .

SUBSTITUTIONS: Use white beans instead of tofu for a similar result. Any berry can replace the blueberries.

Protein: 3.5 g | Fiber: 3.4 g | Fat: 2.3 g | Calories: 108 | Sodium: 40 mg | Carbs: 20.7 g | Sugars: 14.7 g

Aloe Vera Cooler

Drinking straight aloe vera juice is a thing. People drink bottled aloe vera juice regularly for many health benefits including better digestion, clearer skin, reduced heartburn and a more balanced body pH. So I used it to create a hydrating and refreshing drink. It's delicious—much more pleasant to drink than plain aloe vera—and customizable. So what is aloe vera? It's the juice from a succulent plant called aloe. Its list of benefits runs long, but most people partake for its beauty and digestion benefits. Adding orange slices ups the vitamin factor, while sparkling water makes it a fun and more refreshing experience. Cheers!

MAKES 2 (8-OZ [240-ML]) SMOOTHIES

½ cup (120 ml) aloe vera

½ cup (93 g) oranges, peeled

1½ cups (360 ml) sparkling water

3 lime slices

Ice, optional

Add the aloe vera and oranges to a blender and process until the fruit is dispersed. Pour the mixture into a glass and add the sparkling water. Drop in the lime slices. And you might want to add some ice. Enjoy right away.

• •

SUBSTITUTIONS: The only substitution option is the fruit. Feel free to use any juicy fruit that you have on hand.

Protein: 0.4 g | Fiber: 1.1 g | Fat: 0.1 g | Calories: 42 | Sodium: 0 mg | Carbs: 5.4 g | Sugars: 4.3 g

Mayan Chocolate

I had a scoop of ice cream once when I was little that someone told me was Mayan Chocolate and forever more, my association with the phrase was pure bliss. So I tried to recreate that memory and, judging from the swoons of my recipe testers, I think, by Jove, I've got it! The milk, cacao powder, dates and cinnamon are all pretty basic for a healthy chocolate drink. What makes this smoothie Mayan is the green chili pepper. And not from the green part, which has very little bite, but the seeds. Adding five tiny seeds will lead you to chocolate spicy Mayan bliss. This smoothie is notably high in fiber, from the chili pepper, cacao powder and dates.

MAKES 2 (8-OZ [240-ML]) SMOOTHIES

2 cups (480 ml) almond milk

4 tbsp (21 g) cacao powder

3 dates, soaked and pitted

2 tsp (6 g) green chili pepper, chopped, plus 5 seeds

Pinch of ground cinnamon

Pinch of salt

Add all the ingredients to a blender and process until the mixture is smooth. Enjoy immediately, or if you prefer, refrigerate for an hour to give it an extra chill.

· ·

SUBSTITUTIONS: Swap the chili pepper for ground cayenne pepper; you'll have to decide how much is to your taste. Unsweetened cocoa powder can be used instead of cacao powder. Cacao powder is higher in nutrition, however. For quality cacao powder, look for brands like Navitas® Organics, Terrasoul Superfoods, Sunfood™ and Anthony's Goods. Three tablespoons (45 ml) of maple syrup can replace the 3 dates.

Protein: 3.3 g | Fiber: 4.4 g | Fat: 4 g | Calories: 122 | Sodium: 143 mg | Carbs: 23.8 g | Sugars: 14.4 g

Buckwheat Overnight Oats

Buckwheat is considered brain food, since it's high in tryptophan, calcium and magnesium, which support your brain's neurological pathways. It's inexpensive. It's nutritious. It's also hard to find. I typically find it in the bulk bin of Whole Foods or online; look for the brand Anthony's Goods. Buckwheat is worth finding for many reasons. This gluten-free seed has many benefits besides brain support. It reduces inflammation, anxiety and stress, protects against radiative stress from computer and microwave use, has a natural ACE inhibitor that helps reduce blood pressure and even reduces heavy metals and balances blood sugar. So toss some buckwheat in your next smoothie and do your brain and body a favor.

MAKES 2 (8-OZ [240-ML]) SMOOTHIES

1 cup (164 g) buckwheat groats, rinsed and soaked a few hours or overnight

1 cup (150 g) strawberries

½ cup (60 g) apples, not peeled

1 cup (240 ml) milk

1 tsp vanilla extract

Rinse the buckwheat again before adding it and all the other ingredients to a blender. Process until the mixture is smooth.

. . . .

SUBSTITUTIONS: Use cooked quinoa instead of buckwheat groats. Simmer the quinoa using one part quinoa to two parts water. Drain and cool before adding the quinoa to your blender. One cup of quinoa adds 8 grams of protein and 5 grams of fiber. Looking for buckwheat groats online? I recommend the Anthony's Goods brand.

Protein: 4 g | Fiber: 5.1 g | Fat: 2.1 g | Calories: 159 | Sodium: 75 mg | Carbs: 34 g | Sugars: 13.1 g

Tahini Cream Shake

What is tahini? Tahini is simply sesame seed butter. I buy it jarred, but it can be made at home by merely blending sesame seeds until they release their oils and become butter. Adding tahini to a smoothie seems like a no brainer. It's kind of like adding nut butter. It also adds all the goodness of sesame seeds and a creamy, healthy oil. Sesame seeds are quite nutritious and have compounds that strengthen the central nervous system and can specifically cross the blood-brain barrier to enrich the brain. Look for tahini in the nut butter aisle. Quality brands include Whole Foods 365® and Once Again® Nut Butter. I wish I had had a tahini shake when I was taking that organic chemistry exam (see My Path to A Daily Smoothie on page 9).

MAKES 2 (8-OZ [240-ML]) SHAKES

4 tbsp (60 g) tahini

4 dates, soaked and pitted

1 tsp ground cinnamon

1 tsp ground ginger

1½ cups (360 ml) milk

Pinch of salt

Add all the ingredients to a blender and process until the mixture is smooth. Enjoy immediately, or if you prefer, refrigerate for an hour to give it an extra chill.

. . . .

SUBSTITUTIONS: Swap the tahini for another seed or nut butter but do change the name.

Protein: 6.4 g | Fiber: 4.8 g | Fat: 18.1 g | Calories: 276 | Sodium: 140 mg | Carbs: 26.4 g | Sugars: 15.2 g

Vanilla Almond Joy

Vanilla Almond Joy sounds like a dessert and it really tastes like one, even though it contains white potatoes. Why white? Because this smoothie is meant to support weight control, and white potatoes have a secret. When chilled, white potatoes convert to something called "resistant starch." The name refers to starch that resists digestion. Eating resistant starch carries many benefits including prolonged feelings of fullness, a healthy gut and even an immunity boost. This is all a magical tool for those trying to lose weight. The trick is the white potatoes, or the smoothie that contains them, has to be chilled before eating. So make this smoothie, chill for a few hours or even overnight, and enjoy!

MAKES 2 (8-OZ [240-ML]) SMOOTHIES

½ cup (75 g) white potatoes, baked or boiled, and not peeled

1½ cups (360 ml) almond milk

2 tbsp (32 g) almond butter

2 tsp (10 ml) maple syrup

Add all the ingredients to a blender and process until the mixture is smooth. Chill for 2 hours or overnight before drinking to create the resistant starch effect.

. . . .

SUBSTITUTIONS: Swap half the milk for ice to speed up the chilling process, although the smoothie will be a bit more watery once it melts.

Protein: 4.8 g | Fiber: 2.5 g | Fat: 10.9 g | Calories: 186 | Sodium: 109 mg | Carbs: 19.4 g | Sugars: 9.6 g

Hummus Fudge Shake

Hummus is an awesome, protein-packed party dip, but it makes a delicious shake as well. Just blend up garbanzo beans, tahini and milk. Throw in a few chocolate chips and you have a super creamy shake that boasts nearly 10 grams of protein, fueling your brainpower, sustaining your energy and keeping you full. If you leave out the chocolate—which has caffeine—you have a shake that supports sleep. Garbanzo beans are full of tryptophan, an amino acid that raises sleep-supporting serotonin.

MAKES 2 (8-OZ [240-ML]) SHAKES

¼ cup (60 g) garbanzo beans, canned, drained and rinsed

2 tbsp (30 g) tahini

¼ cup (44 g) chocolate chips, melted

1½ cups (360 ml) milk

Pinch of salt

Add all the ingredients to a blender and process until the mixture is smooth. Enjoy immediately, or if you prefer, refrigerate for an hour to give it an extra chill.

· ·

SUBSTITUTIONS: Garbanzo beans can be replaced with white beans, though the flavor will be milder. You can also replace both the garbanzo beans and tahini with ⅓ cup (80 g) of your favorite hummus. Use quality chocolate chips with 70 percent or higher cacao content or just chop up a dark chocolate bar. Quality chocolate brands with minimal ingredients include Enjoy Life®, Theo Chocolate, Chocolove and Hu Kitchen.

Protein: 9.7 g | Fiber: 6.5 g | Fat: 17.7 g | Calories: 338 | Sodium: 145 mg | Carbs: 36.8 g | Sugars: 18.1 g

Goji Berries Booster

Is there anything goji berries can't do? These tiny red berries are available to the Western world as a dehydrated, raisin-like snack or a powder. They are full of protein, fiber, immune-boosting nutrients and my favorite, mood-supporting amino acids. In fact, there is a legend about a town where goji bushes grow on the banks of its water source. It is said that the townspeople are the happiest people on earth, all because their water is rich in goji berry juice. I'll take some of that, thank you.

MAKES 2 (8-OZ [240-ML]) SMOOTHIES

2 tbsp (12 g) goji berry powder

1 cup (123 g) raspberries

½ cup (75 g) cashews, raw and unsalted

1 cup (240 ml) ice water

Add all the ingredients to a blender and process until the mixture is smooth. Enjoy immediately.

. . . .

SUBSTITUTIONS: Swap the raspberries for any other berry, and the cashews for almonds, although the smoothie will be less sweet. For goji berries or powder I recommend the brands Navitas® Organics and Terrasoul Superfoods.

Protein: 7 g | Fiber: 5 g | Fat: 16.3 g | Calories: 259 | Sodium: 36 mg | Carbs: 23.5 g | Sugars: 7.4 g

Mango Sleep Juice

Mangoes make a wonderful sleep aid, did you know? And blending them into a juice with low-glycemic blueberries and spinach is smart and refreshing. Add a splash of lime and some ice and you have a bedtime elixir that will have you counting sheep in no time. How do these ingredients support sleep? Mango is rich in the compound pyridoxine, which drives the production of serotonin and dopamine, relaxants that lead the body into sleep. Leafy greens help the body produce melatonin, the hormone that supports the body's sleep-wake rhythm. Blueberries and lime are there for flavor. Do you need a better sleep tonight?

MAKES 2 (8-OZ [240-ML]) JUICES

½ cup (74 g) blueberries

½ cup (82 g) mango

½ cup (15 g) spinach leaves

2 tbsp (30 ml) lime juice

½ cup (70 g) ice

Add all the ingredients to a blender and process until the mixture is smooth. Pour through a fine sieve and reserve the liquid as your juice. Enjoy right away or refrigerate and drink within 48 hours for optimal nutritional benefit.

NO-WASTE TIP:
The pulp left in the sieve is actually high in nutrition—freeze it and toss it into any smoothie as a boost.

SUBSTITUTIONS: Any leafy greens can be used instead of spinach, including Swiss chard, kale, turnip greens and collard greens. Blackberries can replace the blueberries. For the best sleep support, the mangoes should not be substituted.

Protein: 0.9 g | Fiber: 1.8 g | Fat: 0.3 g | Calories: 53 | Sodium: 7 mg | Carbs: 13.6 g | Sugars: 9.6 g

Cucumber-Mint Juice

Do cucumbers have beauty benefits? Does a spa serve cucumber water? Yes and yes! Cucumbers are popular in skin applications but eating them is insanely healthy. This light, hydrating veggie is rich in B vitamins, which fight aging, are high in silica and sulfur, trigger hair growth and are high in unique antioxidants that are super-strong immunity system boosters. Add these cukes to a blender with electrolyte-rich honeydew and you have a juice that will make you happy with your mirror.

MAKES 2 (8-OZ [240-ML]) JUICES

1 English cucumber, not peeled

½ cup (85 g) honeydew

4 mint leaves

⅔ cup (160 ml) water

Add all the ingredients to a blender and process until the mixture is smooth. Pour through a fine sieve and reserve the liquid as your juice. Enjoy right away or refrigerate and drink within 48 hours for optimal nutritional benefit.

NO-WASTE TIP: The pulp left in the sieve is actually high in nutrition—freeze it and toss it into any smoothie as a boost.

SUBSTITUTIONS: Cantaloupe is a fine substitute for the honeydew.

Protein: 2 g | Fiber: 2.6 g | Fat: 0.4 g | Calories: 48 | Sodium: 18 mg | Carbs: 11.2 g | Sugars: 6 g

Pineapple Calm Shot

Pineapples are fresh and exciting, triggering festive tropical vibes. But did you know they can be calming and even sleep-inducing? Pineapples contain tryptophan, that famed amino acid that triggers sleep-supporting serotonin. Blending this fresh fruit with magnesium-rich spinach and chamomile tea, with its relaxant properties, creates a convenient soothing shot to throw back when you feel stressed or just need to unwind for bed.

MAKES 1 (4-OZ [120-ML]) SHOT

3 tbsp (45 g) pineapple pulp

¼ cup (7 g) spinach leaves

½ cup (120 ml) chamomile tea, freshly brewed and cooled

Add all the ingredients to a blender and process until the mixture is smooth. Pour through a fine sieve, reserving the liquid as your shot. Drink at once or multiply the recipe, pour the shots into ice cube trays and freeze, thawing as you need one.

. . . .

NO-WASTE TIP:
The pulp left in the sieve is actually high in nutrition—freeze it and toss it into any smoothie as a boost.

SUBSTITUTIONS: Any leafy green can replace spinach, and spearmint tea is similar to chamomile in its calming effects.

Protein: 0.4 g | Fiber: 0.6 g | Fat: 0.1 g | Calories: 17 | Sodium: 6 mg | Carbs: 4.3 g | Sugars: 3.1 g

Blue Spirulina Shot

Only nature's magic can explain how spirulina, a tiny single-celled organism, can pack in so many essential vitamins and minerals. As I point out in my Spirulina Mango recipe (page 90), the beautiful blue superfood is so potent, NASA is eyeing it for astronaut nutrition. Spirulina is the perfect addition to your shot rotation because it sucks heavy metals and toxins out of your body and is pumped with protein. Combined with protein-rich hemp seeds, you have a shot with a whopping 12 grams of protein that helps you build and repair tissue, makes enzymes and hormones and runs bodily functions. Protein is the currency your body needs, so down this shot and pat yourself on the back for treating your body so well.

MAKES 1 (4-OZ [120-ML]) SHOT

½ tsp blue spirulina

2 tbsp (20 g) hemp seeds

½ cup (76 g) white grapes

½ cup (120 ml) ice water

Add all the ingredients to a blender and process until the mixture is smooth. Pour through a fine sieve, reserving the liquid as your shot. Drink at once or multiply the recipe, pour the shots into ice cube trays and freeze, thawing as you need one.

NO-WASTE TIP: The pulp left in the sieve is actually high in nutrition—freeze it and toss it into any smoothie as a boost.

SUBSTITUTIONS: Green spirulina works just as well here, and chia seeds can be used instead of hemp. Looking for blue spirulina? I recommend the brand E3Live® Blue Majik®.

Vegetable Harvest:
GARDEN GREEN SMOOTHIES & JUICES

Making smoothies with vegetables is a wonderful way to get in your recommended daily amount of vegetables. The USDA suggests adults eat 2 to 3 cups of vegetables per day. It's easy to meet that requirement, especially with a smoothie.

The benefits of serving up veggies in smoothies are vast.

First off, you can hide them. For a long time, I have hidden zucchini and cauliflower behind beloved melons and berries. Family members, especially the younger additions, rarely suspect the addition of vegetables. More recently, I have branched out, testing out many more veggies to see which I can hide and which don't pass muster for a smoothie. Hiding green peas was a wonderful recent discovery, while the stiff leaves of green cabbage didn't work out so well.

Second, fresh and frozen vegetables are actually less expensive than fruits, so making smoothies that are half veggie and half fruit is more cost effective.

Finally, the nutritional benefits of veggies are off the charts. To smoothies, vegetables add few calories yet an abundance of nutrients, including potassium, protein, fiber, folate and a range of vitamins and essential minerals.

Using vegetables in smoothies also makes it easy to "eat the rainbow," meaning to vary the colors. Often, we try to make a different color every day.

I hope you enjoy my vegetable-based smoothies. Pay close attention to my favorites, which include Ruby Red Beet (page 120), Broccoli Apple (page 122), Rainbow Pepper Juice (page 140) and even my fun invention, an Aquafaba Fizz Shot (page 143), a healthy veggie take on the classic gin fizz cocktail. Happy vegetable hunting!

Chocolate Avocado

A zucchini smoothie hidden behind an avocado-chocolate wall. The avocado provides slow-burning, healthy fats, while the cacao powder ignites your cognitive powers and boosts your mood. Meanwhile, the zucchini is delivering high levels of protein, fiber and minerals essential to supporting feel-good hormones. Are you thinking all this as you are sipping? Nope. All you can taste is this multi-level chocolate flavor, with a hint of mocha. The quintessential hidden veggie smoothie.

MAKES 2 (8-OZ [240-ML]) SMOOTHIES

1 cup (112 g) zucchini, raw and unpeeled

1 avocado, pitted and peeled

1 tbsp (5 g) cacao powder

2 dates, soaked and pitted

2 tbsp (30 ml) brewed coffee

½ cup (120 ml) milk

½ cup (70 g) ice

Add all the ingredients to a blender and process until the mixture is smooth. Enjoy immediately.

· ·

SUBSTITUTIONS: Cauliflower can be used instead of zucchini. Two tablespoons (30 ml) of maple syrup can be used instead of the 2 dates. Unsweetened cocoa powder can be used instead of cacao powder.

Protein: 3.6 g | Fiber: 8.8 g | Fat: 20.7 g | Calories: 259 | Sodium: 48 mg | Carbs: 20.2 g | Sugars: 8.3 g

Zucchini Strawberry

Zucchini is wonderfully humble. It is full of hydrating nutrients, helps support bones, vision, blood pressure, blood sugar levels and even protects against stress. Yet with all the fiber, protein and nutrients it provides, it still doesn't mind taking a backseat to the berries. Here it allows strawberries front-row attention for all the glory of flavor and color. But as you sip this fruity delight, remember it's the presence of magnesium and vitamins B-complex, C and E from zucchini that is working to reduce your stress.

MAKES 2 (8-OZ [240-ML]) SMOOTHIES

½ cup (56 g) zucchini, raw and unpeeled

½ cup (75 g) strawberries

½ cup (76 g) white grapes

¼ cup (65 g) white beans, canned, rinsed and drained

¼ cup (60 ml) milk

Add all the ingredients to a blender and process until the mixture is smooth. Enjoy immediately, or if you prefer, refrigerate for an hour to give it an extra chill.

· ·

SUBSTITUTIONS: Yogurt can replace the white beans and white mushrooms can replace the zucchini. Mango or another stronger-flavored fruit can be used instead of strawberries.

Protein: 6.8 g | Fiber: 5.1 g | Fat: 0.8 g | Calories: 123 | Sodium: 25 mg | Carbs: 23.9 g | Sugars: 7.3 g

Ruby Red Beet

Beets turn everything they touch a lovely shade of pink, including smoothies. For ease of preparation, I simply peel raw beets and toss the chunks into a blender. I know the smoothie I create will be packed with essential nutrients, including fiber, folate, potassium, iron and vitamin C. These specific nutrients are known to increase exercise performance, which in turn supports weight-control efforts. Add in the vitamin C–rich oranges and fiber-packed cauliflower, and I've nearly met my veggie quota for the day. And I've eaten half the rainbow. All before 9 a.m.

MAKES 2 (8-OZ [240-ML]) SMOOTHIES

1 cup (100 g) cauliflower florets

½ cup (93 g) oranges, peeled

½ cup (68 g) beets

½ cup (120 ml) coconut water

For the creamiest result, first steam and cool your cauliflower. Then, add all the ingredients to a blender and process until the mixture is smooth. Enjoy immediately, or if you prefer, refrigerate for an hour to give it an extra chill.

. . . .

SUBSTITUTIONS: Grapes can replace the oranges, while the cauliflower is easily interchangeable with zucchini as a nutritious thickener.

Protein: 2.6 g | Fiber: 3.8 g | Fat: 0.3 g | Calories: 64 | Sodium: 111 mg | Carbs: 14.4 g | Sugars: 10.4 g

Broccoli Apple

Why do some people laugh when I suggest a broccoli smoothie? This one, with sweet apples and creamy, protein-rich garbanzo beans, is a favorite in our house. The apples help mask the green taste of broccoli, and the lime brightens the flavor. Did you know garbanzo beans contain tryptophan, a natural relaxant? This is the perfect smoothie to drink as a nightcap in the evening, broccoli and all.

MAKES 2 (8-OZ [240-ML]) SMOOTHIES

¼ cup (18 g) broccoli

1 cup (120 g) apples, not peeled

¼ cup (7 g) spinach leaves

2 tbsp (30 g) garbanzo beans, canned, drained and rinsed

¼ cup (60 ml) ice water

1 tbsp (15 ml) lime juice

For the creamiest result, first steam and cool your broccoli. Then, add all the ingredients to a blender and process until the mixture is smooth. Enjoy immediately.

. . . .

SUBSTITUTIONS: Pears can replace the apples, cauliflower can replace the broccoli and any leafy green can be used instead of spinach.

Protein: 3.2 g | Fiber: 5.3 g | Fat: 1.1 g | Calories: 110 | Sodium: 12 mg | Carbs: 24 g | Sugars: 13.3 g

Purple Sweet Pea

Sweet peas are a wonderful veggie side dish on the dinner table, but did you know they are excellent support for your nails, hair and complexion? High in vitamin C and other minerals, peas support the body's production of collagen. That's awesome news because collagen keeps skin firm and glowing, hair shining and nails strong. Peas also add protein and a creamy texture. Adding a cup of blueberries adds more toxin-flushing antioxidants and turns the smoothie purple. Pea protein purple power. Say that three times fast.

MAKES 2 (8-OZ [240-ML]) SMOOTHIES

½ cup (72 g) sweet peas

¼ cup (37 g) cashews, raw and unsalted

1 cup (148 g) blueberries

⅔ cup (160 ml) cashew milk

1 tsp ground cinnamon

Add all the ingredients to a blender and process until the mixture is smooth. Enjoy immediately, or if you prefer, refrigerate for an hour to give it an extra chill.

SUBSTITUTIONS: Steamed asparagus tips can be used instead of peas, almonds can replace the cashews and any berry can replace the blueberries.

Protein: 5.1 g | Fiber: 4.1 g | Fat: 9 g | Calories: 178 | Sodium: 58 mg | Carbs: 21.7 g | Sugars: 10.1 g

Sweet Potato Walnut Pie

Sweet potatoes are a festive, comforting root vegetable, whether in a pie, in a cake or in a smoothie. Nutritionally, they are wonders for our vision, skin, immunity and anti-aging. That's because of their abundance of the antioxidant beta-carotene. And they are low in sugar and high in fiber. Add in protein heavyweights nut butter and walnuts and we have a protein party going on. Look for quality nut butter brands like Barney Butter, Justin's® and Whole Foods 365®. The pinch of pumpkin pie spice is the perfect finish to this sweet potato pie turned smoothie.

MAKES 2 (8-OZ [240-ML]) SMOOTHIES

1 sweet potato

2 tbsp (28 g) walnuts

2 tbsp (32 g) almond butter

1 tsp maple syrup

1 cup (240 ml) almond milk

¼ tsp pumpkin pie spice

Healthy Cinnamon Crumble, for topping, optional (see below)

Cook the sweet potato by poking holes into the skin with a fork and microwaving it for 4 to 5 minutes or until it feels soft. Let the potato cool for a few minutes. Scoop out the inside and add it to your blender. Allow it to cool at least 10 minutes.

Add the rest of the ingredients to the blender and process until the drink is smooth. Chill the drink in the refrigerator for an hour. Then, top your smoothie with the Healthy Cinnamon Crumble, if desired, and drink!

BONUS RECIPE:
Healthy Cinnamon Crumble

In your blender, process 2 tablespoons (28 g) of walnuts, 2 tablespoons (20 g) of rolled oats, 3 pitted dates, 1 teaspoon of ground cinnamon and a pinch of salt. Store in a sealed container in the refrigerator for a week.

. . . .

SUBSTITUTIONS: Almonds can replace walnuts. Any nut butter can be used. Want to make the recipe nut free? Use sunflower seed butter instead.

Protein: 6.9 g | Fiber: 4 g | Fat: 15 g | Calories: 236 | Sodium: 92 mg | Carbs: 21.8 g | Sugars: 9.5 g

Purple Cabbage Shake

This is one of those smoothies that doesn't sound like it could taste as good as it does. One recipe tester said it was basically a blueberry muffin shake. Imagine that! A smoothie with purple cabbage tastes like a bakery treat. I was honestly surprised because I had just had a complete recipe fail using green cabbage. But the leaves of purple cabbage are much thinner and easier for a high-speed blender to obliterate, so the resulting smoothie here is a creamy, purple, buttery gem. Oh, and the nutrients that purple cabbage delivers aren't bad either. At every turn, this purple veggie is a fierce inflammation fighter and a huge immunity system booster. Pretty impressive for a smoothie that tastes like a blueberry muffin.

MAKES 2 (8-OZ [240-ML]) SHAKES

¼ cup (18 g) purple cabbage, shredded

½ cup (74 g) blueberries

½ banana, peeled

2 tbsp (32 g) cashew butter

1 cup (240 ml) milk

Add all the ingredients to a blender and process until the mixture is smooth. Enjoy immediately, or if you prefer, refrigerate for an hour to give it an extra chill.

. . . .

SUBSTITUTIONS: Any nut butter would achieve the same flavor and texture. Look for quality nut butter brands like Barney Butter, Justin's® and Whole Foods 365®. Want to make the recipe nut free? Use sunflower seed butter instead. Look for brands like SunButter® and Once Again® Nut Butter. Half of a pear can be used instead of the banana.

Protein: 7 g | Fiber: 2.9 g | Fat: 16.5 g | Calories: 262 | Sodium: 72 mg | Carbs: 24.5 g | Sugars: 12.4 g

Blackberry-Zucchini Splash

Zucchini is working with another remarkable berry in this smoothie. It's the blackberry, and it has little-known health benefits that I feature in this zingy splash! This low-calorie fruit is generally high in vitamin C and fiber, but has some unique strengths as well, including the ability to prevent oral disease and the ability to reduce brain inflammation caused by an accident or aging. Combined with zucchini's fiber and the green chili pepper's snappy seeds, we have a beautiful rose-colored drink that is as refreshing as it is remarkably healthy.

MAKES 2 (8-OZ [240-ML]) SMOOTHIES

¼ cup (28 g) zucchini, raw and unpeeled

½ cup (72 g) blackberries

2 tsp (6 g) green chili pepper, chopped, plus 5 seeds

1¼ cups (300 ml) ice water

Add all the ingredients to a blender and process until the mixture is smooth. Enjoy immediately.

. . . .

SUBSTITUTIONS: Blueberries can replace blackberries but they bring different nutrients. Half a teaspoon of cayenne pepper can replace the green chili pepper and seeds.

Protein: 0.8 g | Fiber: 2.3 g | Fat: 0.3 g | Calories: 20 | Sodium: 2 mg | Carbs: 4.5 g | Sugars: 2.3 g

Berry Soft Serve

Buckwheat groats in a soft serve? Who knew? I love buckwheat groats because they are filling, gluten-free, full of fiber and protein and are an excellent slow-burn energizer. Blending them up with frosty berries seems like a great idea. Both berries up the fiber considerably. To make the buckwheat extra smooth, I soaked it for 20 minutes, rinsed it well and blended it with the berries and milk. So delicious, and the bubblegum-pink color is just fun.

MAKES 2 (8-OZ [240-ML]) SMOOTHIES

½ cup (82 g) buckwheat groats, soaked for 20 minutes and rinsed

½ cup (75 g) strawberries, frozen

½ cup (61 g) raspberries, frozen

¼ cup (60 ml) milk

Add all the ingredients to a blender and process until the mixture is smooth. Enjoy immediately, or if you prefer, refrigerate for an hour to give it an extra chill.

SUBSTITUTIONS: Blueberries and blackberries can be used in place of strawberries and raspberries, but the color, of course, would change.

Protein: 4.5 g | Fiber: 5.7 g | Fat: 1.6 g | Calories: 136 | Sodium: 21 mg | Carbs: 28.6 g | Sugars: 4.7 g

Asparagus Mint

Would you put asparagus in your smoothie? You should! Asparagus is low in calories, since it is mostly water, and extremely high in fiber. All three qualities make it a winner in the weight control category. I love the taste of the tips, and coincidentally, the tips are what work best in a smoothie. I suggest you steam the veggie before blending. Raw asparagus, even the tips, are a bit too tough to break down sufficiently into a creamy smoothie. The pear and kiwi are bright flavors that block any green flavor that might not be pleasing to certain smoothie drinkers. And the mint provides the final fresh spark.

MAKES 2 (8-OZ [240-ML]) SMOOTHIES

6 asparagus tips, steamed

1 pear, cored and chopped

¼ cup (44 g) kiwi

6 mint leaves

¾ cup (180 ml) ice water

Add all the ingredients to a blender and process until the mixture is smooth. Enjoy immediately.

. . . .

SUBSTITUTIONS: More pear can be used instead of kiwi.

Protein: 1.5 g | Fiber: 4 g | Fat: 0.3 g | Calories: 63 | Sodium: 4 mg | Carbs: 15.7 g | Sugars: 9.5 g

ENERGY

Cauliflower Oreo® Shake

You would guess that an Oreo smoothie would be in a dessert category, but this smoothie is actually more creamy than sweet. That's because cauliflower is extraordinary at frothing up a smoothie's texture. Then, we also add yogurt and the whole drink depends on only two Oreos for sweetening. The result is a protein-rich smoothie with minimal sugar yet hints of a childhood friend. Be sure to taste-test and add more Oreos if you'd like, or even a spoonful or two of maple syrup. Enjoy this creamy dream.

MAKES 2 (8-OZ [240-ML]) SMOOTHIES

½ cup (50 g) cauliflower florets

2 Oreos

½ cup (120 ml) almond milk

½ cup (120 ml) yogurt

¼ tsp vanilla extract

Pinch of ground cinnamon

For the creamiest result, first steam and cool your cauliflower. Then, add all the ingredients to a blender and process until the mixture is smooth. Enjoy immediately, or if you prefer, refrigerate for an hour to give it an extra chill.

SUBSTITUTIONS: You can replace the Oreos with a different cookie. The yogurt can be replaced with milk for a thinner texture.

Protein: 4.3 g | Fiber: 0.7 g | Fat: 3.4 g | Calories: 65 | Sodium: 85 mg | Carbs: 7.8 g | Sugars: 16.4 g

Spiced Pumpkin Pie

Pumpkin is one of those surprise vegetables. You know it as a fall-holiday ornament, but it is very nutritious as well. Low in calories, the veggie is especially high in vitamin K, which supports the immune system. Plus, the orange color tells you beta-carotene is present, which delivers vitamin A, a tough infection fighter. But what I love most about this pumpkin pie smoothie is how it tastes just like the holiday pie, thanks to the additions of pear and cinnamon. Canned, unsweetened organic pumpkin puree works well. Don't mistake this for pumpkin pie filling. Look for the organic brand Farmer's Market Foods.

MAKES 2 (8-OZ [240-ML]) SMOOTHIES

1 cup (245 g) pumpkin, canned and unsweetened

½ pear, cored and chopped

1 cup (240 ml) milk

1 tsp ground cinnamon

To make the smoothie, add all the ingredients to a blender and process until the mixture is smooth. Enjoy immediately, or if you prefer, refrigerate for an hour to give it an extra chill.

. . . .

SUBSTITUTIONS: Canned pumpkin can be replaced with canned sweet potato.

Protein: 5.5 g | Fiber: 5.2 g | Fat: 2.9 g | Calories: 126 | Sodium: 64 mg | Carbs: 22.1 g | Sugars: 13 g

Chai Moon Milk

There's something so calming about moon milk. Which is the point, really. Moon milk is based on an ancient tradition that involves drinking a warm beverage to assist sleep. My recipe relies on chai spices for flavor, which are considered stress relieving and conducive for sleep. But I also add a significant amount of hemp seeds to thicken the texture and for sustenance. Hemp seeds are rich in protein and filling up on protein before bed helps you stay asleep and undisturbed by hunger pains. Softly simmering this drink on the stove will also fill your kitchen with delicious, sleep-inducing aromas. Good night.

MAKES 2 (8-OZ [240-ML]) SMOOTHIES

2 tbsp (20 g) hemp seeds

1 tsp chai spices

1½ cups (360 ml) warm milk

½ tsp vanilla extract

Add all the ingredients to a pot on the stove and simmer and stir until the mixture is smooth. Enjoy immediately or refrigerate for later.

. . . .

SUBSTITUTIONS: There are no substitutes for this recipe.

Protein: 5.8 g | Fiber: 0.5 g | Fat: 8.7 g | Calories: 129 | Sodium: 105 mg | Carbs: 7 g | Sugars: 4.5 g

Pomegranate-Rhubarb Shake

Fruity pomegranates are usually paired with other fruity friends like cherries and berries, but I thought it was time to use it in a creamy concoction. And I was right—the sweet, floral tones are showcased beautifully within the cashew-cream base, sweetened with apple. It goes to show you, following usually is not always the best plan. Pomegranates are among the most nutritionally powerful fruits, and thus pump your body with energy. Remember, you break open this pink fruit and scoop out the inner seeds, called arils.

MAKES 2 (8-OZ [240-ML]) SHAKES

½ cup (87 g) pomegranate arils

¼ cup (34 g) rhubarb, chopped and frozen

½ cup (75 g) cashews, raw and unsalted

½ cup (60 g) apples, not peeled

½ cup (120 ml) ice water

Add all the ingredients to a blender and process until the mixture is smooth. Enjoy immediately.

· ·

SUBSTITUTIONS: A pear can be used instead of an apple. Use frozen cucumber instead of the rhubarb for a less tangy flavor.

Protein: 5.5 g | Fiber: 3.7 g | Fat: 16 g | Calories: 305 | Sodium: 11 mg | Carbs: 39.6 g | Sugars: 27.7 g

Chocolate Cauliflower

Cauliflower is considered a complete vegetable, meaning it contains nearly every nutrient essential for overall health. And I consider chocolate essential for overall fun. So this energizing smoothie is the perfect match. The pairing of cacao and cayenne in this smoothie is particularly beneficial for cognitive processes such as attention and focus. That's because the substances in cacao improve blood flow to the brain, while cayenne pepper boosts nutrient delivery. A win-win made even better with chocolate involved.

MAKES 2 (8-OZ [240-ML]) SMOOTHIES

1 cup (100 g) cauliflower florets

2 tbsp (11 g) cacao powder

2 tbsp (30 ml) maple syrup

1 cup (240 ml) milk

Pinch of ground cayenne pepper

For the creamiest result, first steam and cool your cauliflower. Then, add all the ingredients to a blender and process until the mixture is smooth. Enjoy immediately, or if you prefer, refrigerate for an hour to give it an extra chill.

· ·

SUBSTITUTIONS: Black pepper can be used instead of cayenne pepper. Unsweetened cocoa powder can be used instead of cacao powder, although the nutritional boost will be lower. Cacao powder is higher in fiber and magnesium.

Protein: 7.7 g | Fiber: 7.3 g | Fat: 6.1 g | Calories: 161 | Sodium: 54 mg | Carbs: 31 g | Sugars: 17 g

Rainbow Pepper Juice

Are you seeing rainbows? You will once you've tried this juice. Red and green, and even yellow peppers, are overflowing with the primary vitamins your immune system depends on—vitamins A, C and K. These antioxidant vitamins fight disease, help repair aging cells, squash viral invaders and more. And all you have to do to get all this protection is blend, blend, blend and drink. Oh, and this juice definitely tastes better after a chill.

MAKES 2 (8-OZ [240-ML]) JUICES

½ cup (74 g) red, yellow and green bell peppers, chopped

½ cup (77 g) peaches

1 tbsp (5 g) ground ginger

1 tbsp (15 ml) lemon juice

½ cup (120 ml) ice water

Add all the ingredients to a blender and process until the mixture is smooth. Pour through a fine sieve and reserve the liquid as your juice. Enjoy right away or refrigerate and drink within 48 hours for optimal nutritional benefit.

· ·

SUBSTITUTIONS: You can make this juice efficiently with all or one of the pepper colors. A pear can be used instead of a peach.

Protein: 1 g | Fiber: 1.4 g | Fat: 0.4 g | Calories: 35 | Sodium: 3 mg | Carbs: 7.8 g | Sugars: 5.3 g

NO-WASTE TIP:
The pulp left in the sieve is actually high in nutrition—freeze it and toss it into any smoothie as a boost.

Sparkling Grape Juice

Why buy commercial grape juice saturated with refined sugar when you can make your own? My healthy version boasts aloe vera and a hint of licorice flavor from fennel. One reason this beverage is so useful to those trying to lose a few pounds is that fennel is a diuretic, so water weight comes off encouragingly fast. Another is the aloe vera, known for its ability to squash appetites and nix the urge to snack. And the sparkling water adds a refreshing twist.

MAKES 2 (8-OZ [240-ML]) JUICES

½ cup (43 g) fennel

½ cup (76 g) red grapes

1 tbsp (15 ml) aloe vera

¼ lemon, juice and peel

¾ cup (180 ml) sparkling water

Add all the ingredients except the sparkling water to a blender and process until the mixture is smooth. Pour through a fine sieve and reserve the liquid as your juice. Stir the resulting mixture into the sparkling water. Enjoy right away to enjoy the effervescence of the sparkling water before it dissipates.

NO-WASTE TIP:
The pulp left in the sieve is actually high in nutrition—freeze it and toss it into any smoothie as a boost.

SUBSTITUTIONS: Technically, green grapes can be used instead of red but the color will be, well, green. There are no suitable swaps for fennel and aloe vera.

Protein: 0.6 g | Fiber: 1.1 g | Fat: 0.1 g | Calories: 38 | Sodium: 12 mg | Carbs: 9.9 g | Sugars: 6.3 g

Aquafaba Fizz Shot

I think this might be my favorite shot. It is very fun to make, like playing with clouds. Aquafaba, the liquid in a chickpea can, is whipped into a stiff cream and dolloped on the grapefruit juice mixture. It's meant to resemble the egg white concoction in the traditional gin fizz cocktail. Plus, mine is deliciously healthy and alcohol free. This is a recipe for two shots, since you need a full ¼ cup (60 ml) of aquafaba to whip. I highly recommend you give this unusual drink a try on your next home happy hour!

MAKES 2 (4-OZ [120-ML]) SHOTS

¼ cup (60 ml) lime juice

¼ cup (60 ml) grapefruit juice

¼ cup (60 ml) sparkling water

¼ cup (60 ml) aquafaba

Pinch of cream of tartar, optional

Lime slice, for garnish

Add all the ingredients except the aquafaba, cream of tartar and lime slice to a blender, and process until the juice is combined.

Pour the aquafaba in a mixing bowl and mix with a hand mixer for 5 to 7 minutes or until the aquafaba, which looks like egg whites, turns into a stiff whipped cream. A pinch of cream of tartar early on may help speed up the whipped transition.

Once you have your whipped aquafaba, pour the blender drink over ice and dollop on the whip. Adorn with a lime slice and enjoy.

• •

SUBSTITUTIONS: Nope, nothing to see here today.

Protein: 0.5 g | Fiber: 1.1 g | Fat: 0.1 g | Calories: 23 | Sodium: 12 mg | Carbs: 6.4 g | Sugars: 4.3 g

Strawberry-Beet Shot

Beets are back and better than ever. Beets are my favorite because they are awesome skin boosters, immunity protectors and energizers and they turn drinks the best colors. Combining beets with strawberries in a beauty shot is genius because strawberries are bursting with vitamin C, one of the primary skin-protecting vitamins out there. Even zingy black pepper steps in here to protect skin with its vitamin K, which is excellent at supporting skin elasticity.

MAKES 1 (4-OZ [120-ML]) SHOT

¼ cup (37 g) strawberries

1 tbsp (8 g) beet, chopped

1 tbsp (15 ml) lime juice

1 tbsp (15 ml) water

Pinch of black pepper

Add all the ingredients to a blender and process until the mixture is smooth. Pour through a fine sieve, reserving the liquid as your shot. Drink at once or multiply the recipe, pour the shots into ice cube trays and freeze, thawing as you need one.

. . . .

SUBSTITUTIONS: The lime juice is not essential. But the strawberries, beets and black pepper are.

Protein: 1 g | Fiber: 3.1 g | Fat: 0.3 g | Calories: 39 | Sodium: 10 mg | Carbs: 11.6 g | Sugars: 3.8 g

NO-WASTE TIP:
The pulp left in the sieve is actually high in nutrition—freeze it and toss it into any smoothie as a boost.

Daily Decadence:

DESSERT FRAPPES & SHAKES

Welcome to the wild and wonderful world of healthier dessert smoothies! Add one of these daily dessert drinks to your food rotation and stand back to feel the energizing fireworks.

The Licorice Cream Frappe (page 151) tastes like a fancy Italian pastry. The Gingerbread shake (page 170) is a spiced wonder, while the Cookie Dough Crumble shake (page 148) has that fresh-from-the-oven cookie flavor. Yet these decadent treats won't bring on the traditional dessert sugar crash. Nope. The whole food ingredients in these recipes— which include 70 percent dark chocolate, avocado, oats, dates and fresh spices—unite to fuel your brain, support your blood flow, protect your organs and more.

And to add to the fun and games, I've even shared healthy versions of recipes with a nod to Star Wars™ (page 173), a favorite Girl Scout cookie (page 166) and Twix® candy bar (page 171). Enjoy!

Cookie Dough Crumble

Surprisingly, cauliflower provides the perfect vanilla base for this Cookie Dough Crumble milkshake, as well as some awesome fiber one doesn't normally find in a dessert. But that's not the secret behind this delicious cookie dough flavor. Introducing lucuma, a superfood powder made from a Peruvian fruit that actually tastes like a cross between a caramel and a cookie. And lucuma is not just all about flavor; it provides 4 grams of fiber to this recipe. Find lucuma where superfood powders are sold; look for brands like Navitas® Organics, Terrasoul Superfoods and Sunfood™.

MAKES 2 (8-OZ [240-ML]) SMOOTHIES

½ cup (50 g) cauliflower florets

2 tbsp (24 g) lucuma powder

2 dates, soaked and pitted

2 tbsp (32 g) coconut butter, store-bought or homemade (see bonus recipe)

2 cups (480 ml) milk

½ tsp ground cinnamon

½ tsp vanilla extract

For the creamiest result, first steam and cool your cauliflower. Then, add all the ingredients to a blender and process until the mixture is smooth. Enjoy immediately, or if you prefer, refrigerate for an hour to give it an extra chill.

BONUS RECIPE:
Coconut Butter

Blend 1 cup (93 g) of unsweetened, shredded coconut for 4 to 6 minutes until it becomes creamy. Store the resulting butter in a sealed jar, refrigerated, for a month. Add it to toast, use it as a dip, even stir it in your coffee.

. . . .

SUBSTITUTIONS: The coconut butter can be left off, although it carries anti-bacterial nutrients. Use 1 tablespoon (15 ml) of maple syrup to replace 2 tablespoons (24 g) of lucuma. Two tablespoons (30 ml) of maple syrup can also replace the 2 dates.

Protein: 10.7 g | Fiber: 8.3 g | Fat: 23.1 g | Calories: 358 | Sodium: 133 mg | Carbs: 30.6 g | Sugars: 19.8 g

Licorice Cream Frappe

Who knew as I ransacked the red licorice bins at the seaside candy shops all those years that I could have gotten the same haunting flavor biting into a white, bulb-like veggie named fennel? Well, I know now, and since fennel and the spice anise are similar in flavor, I add them both to smoothies that I want to taste like candy. It's not just fun and games with these two: Both fennel and anise are natural anti-microbials, boosting the power of the body's own immune system. Fennel also has the added power of producing sleep-inducing serotonin, so if you have a hankering for a sweet shake, but also want to take a nap, this Licorice Cream Frappe is calling your name.

MAKES 2 (8-OZ [240-ML]) SMOOTHIES

¼ cup (22 g) fennel bulb, chopped

½ star anise, crushed

1 banana, peeled

1 tbsp (9 g) white sesame seeds

1½ cups (360 ml) milk

½ tsp vanilla extract

½ tsp ground cinnamon

Add all the ingredients to a blender and process until the mixture is smooth. Enjoy immediately, or if you prefer, refrigerate for an hour to give it an extra chill.

. . . .

SUBSTITUTIONS: There really is no swap for fennel and anise, unless you want to use red licorice (only kidding). Two pears can be used instead of the banana.

Protein: 8.4 g | Fiber: 3 g | Fat: 8 g | Calories: 195 | Sodium: 94 mg | Carbs: 25.6 g | Sugars: 15.5 g

Peanut Butter S'more

Who's up for an ice-cold peanut butter s'more jar? This festive jar is basically a blended dessert smoothie, with a creamy base that mimics marshmallows in fluff and sweetness, plus adds a bonus ripple of chocolate and peanut butter. There is a lot of talk this decade about the nutrition in nut butter. Surprisingly, peanuts are often not included. But peanut butter, when made straight from peanuts, is a terrific protein-based energy source, providing 12 grams of protein in just a few tablespoons. It's low in carbs, high in healthy fats and has eye-popping levels of niacin, which boosts the brain and immune system. Look for quality nut butter brands Barney Butter, Justin's® and Whole Foods 365®. So build your peanut butter s'more in a jar and boast about your healthy s'more smoothie.

MAKES 2 (8-OZ [240-ML]) SMOOTHIES

1 pear, cored and chopped

3 tbsp (16 g) cacao powder

3 tbsp (48 g) peanut butter, plus more to drizzle

2 tbsp (30 ml) maple syrup

1 cup (240 ml) almond milk

½ tsp vanilla extract

Pinch of ground cinnamon

Healthy Caramel Sauce, to drizzle, optional (see bonus recipe)

Add all the ingredients to a blender and process until the mixture is smooth. Enjoy immediately, or if you prefer, refrigerate for an hour to give it an extra chill.

Dress It Up: Melt some peanut butter in the microwave to create a drizzle to put on top just before eating. Or make Healthy Caramel Sauce (see below).

BONUS RECIPE: Healthy Caramel Sauce

Soak 15 Medjool (or 30 Deglet Noor) dates overnight and then rinse and pit them. Add them to your blender along with ¼ cup (60 ml) of milk and ½ teaspoon of vanilla extract. Store in a sealed container in the refrigerator for 2 weeks or freeze for 6 months.

· ·

SUBSTITUTIONS: Trade the cacao powder and maple syrup for ¼ cup (44 g) of chocolate chips melted in the microwave for 60 seconds. A banana can replace the pear. Use your own choice of milk. Want to make the recipe nut free? Use sunflower seed butter instead. Look for brands like SunButter® and Once Again® Nut Butter.

Protein: 12.8 g | Fiber: 12.6 g | Fat: 19.5 g | Calories: 338 | Sodium: 183 mg | Carbs: 47.7 g | Sugars: 23.9 g

Cinnamon Snickerdoodle

Another cookie smoothie calling for lucuma powder. This smoothie has another ingredient that will have your taste buds say "Snickerdoodle!" Can you guess? Bakers will know it. It's cream of tartar— but only a smidgen, mind you. That's all you need to unearth that delicious fresh-from-the-oven snickerdoodle flavor. Oh, and of course cinnamon is here, and cashews for the protein-rich sweet cream base. All the regulars have shown up for this snickerdoodle smoothie party.

MAKES 2 (8-OZ [240-ML]) SMOOTHIES

1 cup (150 g) cashews, raw and unsalted

2 tbsp (24 g) lucuma powder

1 cup (120 g) apples, not peeled

¼ tsp cream of tartar

1 tsp ground cinnamon

1 cup (240 ml) milk

½ cup (70 g) ice

Add all the ingredients to a blender and process until the mixture is smooth. Enjoy immediately, or if you prefer, refrigerate for an hour to give it an extra chill.

. . . .

SUBSTITUTIONS: Maple syrup can be used to replace lucuma powder; use only 1 tablespoon (15 ml) of maple syrup to replace 2 tablespoons (24 g) of lucuma. A pear can be used instead of an apple.

Protein: 10.8 g | Fiber: 7.4 g | Fat: 19.5 g | Calories: 475 | Sodium: 12 mg | Carbs: 43 g | Sugars: 16.1 g

Whipped Coffee Tiramisu

Making an energizing coffee smoothie flavored similarly to the Italian treat tiramisu is easy and healthier than the full tiramisu pastry with all those rich layers. My pastry-turned-smoothie version has a bit of protein and is lower in sugar than the international treat. But you can up the sugary decadence if you so choose by topping with a Trendy Dalgona Coffee (bonus recipe below)!

MAKES 2 (8-OZ [240-ML]) SMOOTHIES

1 cup (240 ml) coffee with milk, to taste

1 tbsp (6 g) graham crackers

1 tbsp (11 g) chocolate chips

Ice cubes, for serving

¼ cup (60 ml) whipped cream or optional Trendy Dalgona Coffee (see bonus recipe)

Cacao powder, for serving

Make a cup of coffee and add milk to taste. The coffee can be warm. Add the coffee, graham crackers and chocolate chips to a blender, and process until the mixture is smooth. Pour the coffee smoothie over ice cubes. Spoon the whipped cream over your smoothie, or if desired, make and top with the Trendy Dalgona Coffee whip (see below). Dust with cacao powder and enjoy immediately.

BONUS RECIPE:
Trendy Dalgona Coffee

If you're feeling extra fancy, add 2 tablespoons (6 g) of instant coffee, 2 tablespoons (25 g) of coconut palm sugar and 2 tablespoons (30 ml) of boiling water to a clean bowl. Using a hand mixer, whip it for 2 to 5 minutes until you achieve a stiff coffee-colored whipped texture. Dollop this on your drink!

• •

SUBSTITUTIONS: You can replace the graham crackers and chocolate chips with other cookie and chocolate types. If you make the dalgona coffee, you must use instant coffee—it is the ingredient that creates the telltale froth. You can, however, use cane sugar instead of coconut palm sugar.

Protein: 2.8 g | Fiber: 0.3 g | Fat: 6.5 g | Calories: 83 | Sodium: 25 mg | Carbs: 5.6 g | Sugars: 3.5 g

Cardamom Date

Spices are so often found in cold weather holiday desserts that they are an unexpected delight when encountered in a cool, creamy smoothie. The fiber, of course, comes from the cauliflower and apple. And the flavor is spicy strong, washing over you like a warm wave on a sunny beach. Cardamom is especially pronounced here, likely because dates tend to amplify the flavor. Try to gather all these spices or at least dig up some pumpkin pie spice to allow this smoothie to sing its full flavor.

MAKES 2 (8-OZ [240-ML]) SMOOTHIES

½ cup (50 g) cauliflower florets

2 dates, soaked and pitted

1 cup (120 g) apples, not peeled

1 cup (240 ml) water

¼ tsp ground cardamom

1 tsp ground cinnamon

¼ tsp ground cloves

For the creamiest result, first steam and cool your cauliflower. Then, add all the ingredients to a blender and process until the mixture is smooth. Enjoy immediately, or if you prefer, refrigerate for an hour to give it an extra chill.

• •

SUBSTITUTIONS: A pear can replace the apple. Milk can be used instead of water for a creamier drink.

Protein: 1 g | Fiber: 4.1 g | Fat: 6.5 g | Calories: 88 | Sodium: 9 mg | Carbs: 23.1 g | Sugars: 17.5 g

Raspberry-Chocolate Swirl

This creamy chocolate smoothie is bursting with 10 grams of protein, about one-fifth of the recommended daily need. The protein largely comes from nutty, delicious hemp seeds. They also contribute a creamy texture. Here the avocado and yogurt also contribute a thick texture, so this smoothie can actually be eaten with a spoon.

MAKES 2 (8-OZ [240-ML]) SMOOTHIES

2 cups (246 g) raspberries, divided

½ cup (87 g) chocolate chips

2 tbsp (20 g) hemp seeds

⅔ cup (160 ml) yogurt

2 tbsp (30 ml) maple syrup

Add all the ingredients except ½ cup (62 g) of raspberries to a blender and process until the mixture is smooth. Crush the remaining raspberries with the back of a spoon and swirl into the chocolate smoothie mixture. Enjoy immediately, or if you prefer, refrigerate for an hour to give it an extra chill.

. . . .

SUBSTITUTIONS: Blueberries or strawberries can be used instead of raspberries. Milk can be used instead of yogurt. Use quality chocolate chips with 70 percent or higher cacao content, or just chop up a dark chocolate bar. Quality chocolate brands with minimal ingredients include Enjoy Life®, Theo Chocolate, Chocolove and Hu Kitchen.

Protein: 10.7 g | Fiber: 13.3 g | Fat: 29.9 g | Calories: 475 | Sodium: 37 mg | Carbs: 45 g | Sugars: 27.3 g

Vanilla Birthday Cake

The best way to create a vanilla birthday cake smoothie base is to start with cashews and pears. Soak the cashews overnight to encourage a creamy blend, and core, chop but don't peel the pear for extra fiber. Cashews and zucchini are known for their ability to stave off stress with their high vitamin B6 levels. Vitamin B6 stimulates the body's production of norepinephrine, sometimes called a happy hormone. Potassium also pulls stress down by impacting your body's water balance. This smoothie contributes 10 percent of your daily requirement! And bonus, if you smile while holding this colorful creamy vanilla birthday cake smoothie, smiling is also a scientifically proven de-stressor.

MAKES 2 (8-OZ [240-ML]) SMOOTHIES

½ cup (75 g) cashews, raw and unsalted

1 pear, cored and chopped

¼ cup (28 g) zucchini, raw and unpeeled

½ cup (120 ml) milk

½ cup (70 g) ice

¼ tsp vanilla extract

Pinch of salt

Sprinkles, optional

For a creamier texture, soak the cashews for 4 hours or boil them for 5 minutes and then rinse them. Add all the ingredients to a blender and process until the mixture is smooth. Enjoy immediately.

. . . .

SUBSTITUTIONS: Walnuts can be used instead of cashews for a nuttier flavor. And a banana can be used instead of the pear. A banana can also be used to replace the zucchini, although the flavor will be much sweeter.

Protein: 9.3 g | Fiber: 4 g | Fat: 27 g | Calories: 382 | Sodium: 46 mg | Carbs: 31.6 g | Sugars: 11.4 g

Strawberry Shortcake

This creamy Strawberry Shortcake smoothie has chunks of strawberries and a fruity top. Drink this one during strawberry season so the berries are sweet. Strawberries are high in vitamin C, the most powerful immunity booster among berries. More nutrients come from the pear and flaxseed, but the most powerful immunity boost comes from the tiny tomatoes, which you can't taste here but deliver powerful amounts of disease-fighting lycopene. Top this luscious glass with the Healthy Cinnamon Crumble (page 125) if desired.

MAKES 2 (8-OZ [240-ML]) SMOOTHIES

1 cup (150 g) strawberries, plus more for topping

1 tbsp (7 g) flaxseed

4 cherry tomatoes

1 pear, cored and chopped

¼ cup (60 ml) yogurt

¼ cup (60 ml) milk

Healthy Cinnamon Crumble (page 125), for topping, optional

Add all the ingredients to a blender and process until the mixture is smooth. Enjoy immediately, or if you prefer, refrigerate for an hour to give it an extra chill. Top with extra strawberries and, if desired, Healthy Cinnamon Crumble (page 125).

. . . .

SUBSTITUTIONS: Strawberries cannot be substituted, obvs! But you can leave out the flaxseed and cherry tomatoes, though it's a shame. And an apple or banana can replace the pear.

Protein: 4.4 g | Fiber: 4 g | Fat: 2.4 g | Calories: 124 | Sodium: 41 mg | Carbs: 21.8 g | Sugars: 14.4 g

Blizzard Smoothie

A healthy, ice-cold, clean-slate smoothie for you to sling in as many mix-ins as you want. I get you started with a delicious vanilla base and weight-friendly ingredients including tofu, zucchini and fiber-rich dates. Throw on some cacao nibs and a few cherries, drizzle with melted chocolate and even go a little wild and top with the Healthy Brown Sugar Crumble, if desired, from the bonus recipe below.

MAKES 2 (8-OZ [240-ML]) SMOOTHIES

½ cup (124 g) tofu

½ cup (56 g) zucchini, raw and not peeled

3 dates, soaked and pitted

3 tbsp (18 g) graham crackers, crushed

¼ tsp vanilla extract

½ cup (120 ml) milk

½ cup (70 g) ice

Healthy Brown Sugar Crumble (see bonus recipe), for topping, optional

Whipped cream, for topping, optional

Add all the ingredients to a blender and process until the mixture is smooth. Top with the Healthy Brown Sugar Crumble and whipped cream, if desired. Enjoy immediately.

BONUS RECIPE: Healthy Brown Sugar Crumble

Want to top your smoothie with a bit more pizzazz? In your blender, process 2 tablespoons (28 g) of walnuts, 2 tablespoons (20 g) of rolled oats, 3 pitted dates, 1 teaspoon of coconut palm sugar (or brown sugar) and a pinch of salt. Store in a sealed container in the refrigerator for a week.

. . . .

SUBSTITUTIONS: Use yogurt instead of tofu. Or use 1 tablespoon (15 ml) of maple syrup for each date. Choose your own toppings.

Protein: 6.6 g | Fiber: 2.1 g | Fat: 4.2 g | Calories: 134 | Sodium: 93 mg | Carbs: 19.5 g | Sugars: 12.8 g

Cherry Melba

This festive, cherry twist on a traditional European peach dessert is far healthier than the sugar-laden dessert invented in 1892 to honor the Australian soprano Nellie Melba. Here, cherries and peaches provide the sweet flavor, and together with cacao powder, about 6 grams of fiber, nearly one-fourth of our daily need. Coconut milk provides a creamy base and extra nutrients such as the healthy fat lauric acid, which helps boost immunity. An elegant dessert that supplies a nutritional boost.

MAKES 2 (8-OZ [240-ML]) SMOOTHIES

1 cup (154 g) cherries, pitted

¼ cup (39 g) peaches

1 tbsp (5 g) cacao powder

½ cup (120 ml) coconut milk, canned

1 tbsp (15 ml) maple syrup

½ cup (70 g) ice, optional

Add all the ingredients except the ice to a blender and process until the mixture is smooth. To chill, add ice and blend again or refrigerate for an hour before drinking.

. . . .

SUBSTITUTIONS: Raspberries and strawberries can be used instead of cherries, and the cacao powder can be left off for a vanilla fruit melba version. Unsweetened cocoa can be used instead of cacao powder.

Protein: 4.6 g | Fiber: 6.1 g | Fat: 16.6 g | Calories: 241 | Sodium: 10 mg | Carbs: 27.8 g | Sugars: 19.2 g

Chocolate Cherry

Cherries are rich in sleep-supporting melatonin, so why would I use them in an energy smoothie? Because when paired with chocolate, this team pushes you off the launching pad. Together they increase the bioavailability of essential nutrients, especially potassium, magnesium and other compounds the body needs to operate optimally. That's why eating a cherry chocolate bar before a marathon is such a thing. So why not have a chocolate cherry smoothie instead, before a marathon, or just to energize you for your busy day?

MAKES 2 (8-OZ [240-ML]) SMOOTHIES

½ cup (75 g) cashews, raw and unsalted

1 cup (154 g) cherries, pitted

½ cup (87 g) chocolate chips

½ cup (120 ml) milk

½ cup (70 g) ice

For a creamier texture, soak the cashews for 4 hours or boil them for 5 minutes and then rinse. Add all the ingredients to a blender and process until the mixture is smooth. Enjoy immediately.

. . . .

SUBSTITUTIONS: If you can't find cherries, açai would work perfectly here because, like cherries, açai and chocolate complement each other nutritionally.

Protein: 9.5 g | Fiber: 3.7 g | Fat: 29.2 g | Calories: 475 | Sodium: 76 mg | Carbs: 47.6 g | Sugars: 31.4 g

Samoa Cookie

This Samoa Cookie smoothie is a healthier spin on the flavors of the famed Girl Scout cookie by the same name. The coconut milk is high in healthy fats and other nutrients such as magnesium, which supports proper brain functioning. Walnuts also provide brain-boosting nutrients, and the drink is full of protein—nearly 10 grams—as well as fiber, iron, potassium and even phosphorous, which is vital for healthy bones and teeth. The coconut milk represents the traditional cookie's quintessential coconut flavor, but it packs on calories, so I kept it low. Dates are used here as a sweetener and a drizzle to represent the Girl Scout cookie's ubiquitous caramel drizzle.

MAKES 2 (8-OZ [240-ML]) SMOOTHIES

½ cup (120 ml) coconut milk, canned

½ cup (58 g) walnuts

3 dates, soaked and pitted

¼ cup, plus 3 tsp (55 g) chocolate chips, divided

½ cup (120 ml) ice water

Healthy Caramel Sauce (page 152), for topping, optional

Add the coconut milk, walnuts, dates, ¼ cup (44 g) of chocolate chips and ice water to a blender, and process until the mixture is smooth. Melt 3 teaspoons (11 g) of chocolate chips to drizzle on top or drizzle with Healthy Caramel Sauce. Enjoy immediately, or if you prefer, refrigerate for an hour to give it an extra chill.

· ·

SUBSTITUTIONS: Your choice of milk can replace the coconut milk. Three tablespoons (45 ml) of maple syrup can replace the 3 dates.

Protein: 9.6 g | Fiber: 4.6 g | Fat: 34.4 g | Calories: 394 | Sodium: 14 mg | Carbs: 18.9 g | Sugars: 12.9 g

Lemon Poppy Seed

Drink your lemon poppy seed muffin in a glass this morning and boost your chances of fighting that spring cold. That's because lemon peel is included in this smoothie, not just juice and pulp. A powerful idea as the peel packs calcium, potassium and a compound called D-limonene, all of which support not only the immune system but also many essential body functions. Plus adding the rind helps this smoothie smell incredibly lemony, which actually imposes an immune-boosting, calming effect on your nervous system.

MAKES 2 (8-OZ [240-ML]) SMOOTHIES

1 lemon, juice and pulp, plus ½ the rind

1 tsp lime juice

1 peach, pitted and chopped

1 tsp poppy seeds

¾ cup (180 ml) milk

¼ cup (35 g) ice

Add all the ingredients to a blender and process until the mixture is smooth. Enjoy immediately.

· ·

SUBSTITUTIONS: Orange juice can be used instead of lime juice—this ingredient is meant to cut the sourness of the lemon. A pear or apple can replace the peach.

Protein: 1.6 g | Fiber: 2.2 g | Fat: 1.6 g | Calories: 66 | Sodium: 36 mg | Carbs: 13.9 g | Sugars: 9.8 g

Gingerbread

Who knew the gingerbread man could put you to sleep? The signature flavor of anything gingerbread is, yes, ground ginger, but also molasses. Blackstrap molasses, to be exact. And molasses is rich in magnesium, the golden ticket to a beautiful, sound sleep. Rolled oats support sleep as well by helping you feel full before bed and providing sustained energy through the night so you don't pop up looking for a snack. The quintessential gingerbread spice blend helps the smoothie taste gingerbready, however, if you can't find all the spices, just use cinnamon.

MAKES 2 (8-OZ [240-ML]) SMOOTHIES

1 tsp blackstrap molasses

½ cup (60 g) apples, not peeled

½ cup (45 g) rolled oats

1 tsp gingerbread spice or a blend of ginger, cinnamon, nutmeg, cloves and allspice

1 cup (240 ml) milk

Add all the ingredients to a blender and process until the mixture is smooth. Enjoy immediately, or if you prefer, refrigerate for an hour to give it an extra chill.

. . . .

SUBSTITUTIONS: A pear can replace the apple. Cinnamon can replace the gingerbread spice blend.

Protein: 3.3 g | Fiber: 3.4 g | Fat: 2.7 g | Calories: 146 | Sodium: 73 mg | Carbs: 28 g | Sugars: 10.9 g

Twix® Bar Smoothie

Almond flour in a smoothie adds protein, texture, few calories and a cookie taste. Mix in dates, chocolate and vanilla to create this Twix® Bar Smoothie. Twix bars are a commercial candy made with cookie and caramel. Here, the dates carry the caramel flavor and add iron and other energy-boosting nutrients. So the next time you search for a candy bar to help you cope with the afternoon slump, mix up a Twix® Bar Smoothie instead.

MAKES 2 (8-OZ [240-ML]) SMOOTHIES

½ cup (60 g) almond flour

2 dates, soaked and pitted

¼ cup (44 g) chocolate chips

¾ cup (180 ml) milk

¾ cup (105 g) ice

½ tsp vanilla extract

Add all the ingredients to a blender and process until the mixture is smooth. Enjoy immediately, or if you prefer, refrigerate for an hour to give it an extra chill.

· ·

SUBSTITUTIONS: Use macadamia nuts instead of almond flour for a different buttery flavor. Half of a frozen banana can replace the ¾ cup (105 g) of ice for a thicker, sweeter flavor and even more energy.

Protein: 6.3 g | Fiber: 2.1 g | Fat: 11.6 g | Calories: 225 | Sodium: 60 mg | Carbs: 24.8 g | Sugars: 20.6 g

Blue Bantha™ Milk

Let's duck into Star Wars for a moment and consider drinking milk that is blue. My yummy, creamy version is a plant-based, rich-in-quality protein thanks to the blue algae spirulina and even has a little hidden veggie thrown in. Did they have vegetable gardens on planet Batuu™? The taste of my recipe might differ slightly from the version so many galaxies far, far away. The banana, cauliflower and milk make it so creamy and sweet. The blue spirulina creates that gorgeous hue but thankfully its flavor, rather strong, is undetectable behind a fresh banana. May the force be with you.

MAKES 2 (8-OZ [240-ML]) SMOOTHIES

¼ cup (25 g) cauliflower florets

1 tsp blue spirulina

1 banana, peeled

¼ cup (41 g) mango

1 cup (240 ml) milk

1 tsp lemon juice

For the creamiest result, first steam your cauliflower. Then, add all the ingredients to a blender and process until the mixture is smooth. Enjoy immediately, or if you prefer, refrigerate for an hour to give it an extra chill.

• •

SUBSTITUTIONS: The mango isn't really necessary. The banana can be replaced with a pear. Looking for blue spirulina? I recommend the brand E3Live's® Blue Majik®.

Protein: 3.6 g | Fiber: 2.3 g | Fat: 1.8 g | Calories: 109 | Sodium: 112 mg | Carbs: 22.1 g | Sugars: 13.5 g

Chocolate Crunch

Do you know what this is? A healthy spin on a rice crispy bar turned into a smoothie. But homemade means the only ingredients in your crispy bar smoothie are unsweetened cereal, chocolate chips, cashew butter and milk. The trick to making this smoothie super healthy is to use the purest cereal. I use kasha, which is high in fiber and protein. But you can use your favorite cereal. I'm flexible.

MAKES 2 (8-OZ [240-ML]) SMOOTHIES

½ cup (90 g) kasha cereal

¼ cup (44 g) chocolate chips

2 tbsp (32 g) cashew butter

1¼ cups (300 ml) cashew milk

Add all the ingredients to a blender and process until the mixture is smooth. Enjoy immediately, or if you prefer, refrigerate for an hour to give it an extra chill.

SUBSTITUTIONS: Any nut butter can replace the cashew butter. Look for quality nut butter brands like Barney Butter, Justin's® and Whole Foods 365®. Want to make the recipe nut free? Use sunflower seed butter instead. Look for brands like Sunbutter® and Once Again® Nut Butter. And remember to use a nut-free milk. Use your own cereal, but something with a crunch tastes best in this smoothie.

Protein: 4.7 g | Fiber: 1.2 g | Fat: 15.4 g | Calories: 237 | Sodium: 119 mg | Carbs: 21 g | Sugars: 10.8 g

Black Bean Brownie

Eating a brownie is always a good idea, especially a homemade one. And that applies to brownie smoothies as well, especially this one. Particularly if you are looking to support your skin. That's because this brownie smoothie is made primarily from black beans. And black beans contain anthocyanin, a powerful antioxidant that literally bats away toxins and other forces that hurt or age skin cells. And while I target beauty in this smoothie, the whopping protein and fiber levels—both at 18.5 grams—make this smoothie a general nutritional powerhouse.

MAKES 2 (8-OZ [240-ML]) SMOOTHIES

½ cup (86 g) black beans, canned, rinsed and drained

3 tbsp (16 g) cacao powder

2 tbsp (22 g) chocolate chips

1 cup (176 g) kiwi

1¼ cups (300 ml) milk

Add all the ingredients to a blender and process until the mixture is smooth. Enjoy immediately, or if you prefer, refrigerate for an hour to give it an extra chill.

. . . .

SUBSTITUTIONS: Any creamy, sweet fruit can be used instead of kiwi—think apple, pear, plum, peach. The use of two types of chocolate works to make this smoothie taste like a brownie. Unsweetened cocoa powder can be used instead of cacao powder.

Protein: 18.5 g | Fiber: 18.5 g | Fat: 13.5 g | Calories: 381 | Sodium: 91 mg | Carbs: 64.8 g | Sugars: 15.2 g

Smoothies Transformed into Frozen Treats

A smoothie is a frosty, delicious route to feeling full and building on your daily nutrition. You can get the same benefits from the beverage in a different form—molded into a popsicle, whipped into ice cream, frozen into an icy granita and even shaped into a chocolate-coated treat.

You can still drink these recipes as traditional smoothies, but if you want to experience a smoothie served up in a different form, I've got you covered.

Both my Blackberry–Roasted Peach Smoothie (page 180) and my hidden-veggie Green Smoothie (page 183) make refreshing popsicles. My Ginger-Cinnamon Smoothie (page 178) converts easily to a spicy sweet ice cream. My Strawberry-Balsamic Smoothie (page 181) transforms into a refreshing, flaky granita. Finally, perhaps the most unusual smoothie transformation is my Pineapple Chocolate Magnum® Smoothie (page 184), a twist on a familiar Disney DOLE Whip treat.

Let's create delicious smoothies of a different form!

Ginger-Cinnamon Smoothie Ice Cream

The marriage of ginger and cinnamon creates a bright flavor and a top immunity booster!
The cinnamon spice cradles the pungent ginger in a drink that will balance your blood sugar,
cleanse your system and power your immune system. The fat level is high with healthy fats, including
medium-chain triglycerides from coconut milk, which are known to support many body processes,
as well as boost energy and endurance. As either a smoothie or a creamy ice cream, the first spicy sip
or spoonful provides a bright and surprising burst of warmth. It's easy to make this smoothie as a no-
churn ice cream. Just blend, pour the mixture into a loaf pan, freeze, thaw and scoop as a soft serve.

MAKES 1 (16-OZ [480-ML]) SMOOTHIE OR 1 (16-0Z [454-G]) TUB ICE CREAM

1 cup (240 ml) coconut milk, canned

1 tbsp (15 ml) maple syrup, plus more as necessary

2 tbsp (12 g) fresh ginger, peeled and chopped

2 tbsp (10 g) ground cinnamon

½ cup (120 ml) ice water

1 tsp vanilla extract

Ice cubes, for serving, optional

Blend the ingredients until smooth. Taste test and add more maple syrup as necessary, a teaspoon at a time.

To drink as a smoothie, pour over a few ice cubes and enjoy right away.

To eat as ice cream, pour the mixture into a parchment-lined loaf pan. Cover the top with plastic wrap touching the surface. Freeze for at least 4 hours. Allow the mixture 10 to 15 minutes to thaw before you scoop as a soft serve. Store the mixture in a sealed container in the freezer for a month.

Protein: 3.5 g | Fiber: 6.9 g | Fat: 29 g | Calories: 338 | Sodium: 21 mg | Carbs: 22.7 g | Sugars: 10.3 g

Blackberry-Roasted Peach Smoothie Popsicles

Blackberries and peaches are wonderfully high in fiber and roasting the peaches brings a warm caramel flavor to the recipe. Whip it up in a blender and serve it cold as a smoothie. Or pour the smoothie into a popsicle mold and freeze to enjoy as flavorful, fruity popsicles.

MAKES 1 (16-OZ [480-ML]) SMOOTHIE OR 8 POPSICLES

1 cup (154 g) peaches, sliced, plus more for topping popsicles

1 tbsp (5 g) ground cinnamon

1 cup (144 g) blackberries

1 cup (240 ml) yogurt

Milk, optional

Ice cubes, for serving, optional

Preheat your oven to 375°F (190°C). Spread the peach slices on a cookie sheet. Sprinkle them lightly with the cinnamon, put them in the oven and roast them for about 20 minutes. Allow them to cool, then put them in a blender with the other ingredients.

Blend the ingredients until smooth. You may have to add a bit of milk to loosen up the mixture depending on your yogurt's consistency.

To drink as a smoothie, pour the smoothie over a few ice cubes and enjoy right away.

To make popsicles, pour the mixture into popsicle molds and sprinkle the tops with extra chopped peaches. Freeze the popsicles for just 30 minutes, and then insert the popsicle sticks. Then, freeze the popsicles for at least 4 hours or overnight.

To remove the popsicles from the mold, run hot water over the outside of the popsicle mold and tug at the stick. Take care not to get any water onto the popsicle itself. Store the popsicles in the freezer in a sealed container for 3 months.

Protein: 8.7 g | Fiber: 5 g | Fat: 2.1 g | Calories: 148 | Sodium: 86 mg | Carbs: 22.5 g | Sugars: 19.1 g

Strawberry-Balsamic Smoothie Granita

The indelible flavors of balsamic vinegar and strawberries produce a smoothie that will leave an imprint on your memory. Drink as a beverage or take steps to create the Italian frozen ice delicacy called a granita, which is basically flavorful flaked ice. Either way, your energy levels will soar thanks to the carbs and fruit sugars from strawberries, vitamin C from lemon juice and oxidation reactions from balsamic vinegar. Serve as a refreshing granita for a dry yet crunchy treat both sophisticated enough for dinner parties and reminiscent of childhood snow cones.

MAKES 1 (16-OZ [480-ML]) SMOOTHIE OR 2 CUPS (388 G) OF GRANITA

4 cups (600 g) strawberries

2 tsp (10 ml) lemon juice

½ tsp balsamic vinegar

1 cup (240 ml) water

¼ cup (50 g) cane sugar

To drink as a smoothie, blend all the ingredients except the sugar. Taste the mixture and add only the amount of sugar you need. It will depend on the sweetness of your strawberries.

To consume as a granita, blend all the ingredients, including the sugar, which is needed in a granita to support crystallization. Then, pour the mixture into a shallow baking dish so it reaches about 1-inch (2.5-cm) deep.

Freeze the dish uncovered and every 45 minutes take the dish out and scrape up the mixture with a fork. Re-freeze between each scraping, until the granita is a mound of crystals. It will probably take you three to four scrapings to reach that point.

Serve immediately in small bowls or store the granita crystals in a sealed container in the freezer for a week.

Protein: 2.1 g | Fiber: 6.1 g | Fat: 1 g | Calories: 129 | Sodium: 4 mg | Carbs: 31.5 g | Sugars: 23 g

Green Smoothie Popsicles

These Green Smoothie Popsicles taste sweet and creamy and are full of hidden veggies including avocado and spinach leaves—yes, spinach leaves in a popsicle!—that will go undetected in these homemade, whole food, dairy-free popsicles. The nutrients in the yogurt, avocado and spinach leaves work together in an orchestra of support for hair, skin, nails and more. The avocado boosts the healthy fat levels, and the yogurt and milk hike protein levels, supporting cell replenishment and anti-aging processes.

MAKES 1 (16-OZ [480-ML]) SMOOTHIE OR 8 POPSICLES

1 avocado, pitted and peeled

½ cup (15 g) spinach leaves

1 cup (240 ml) yogurt

3 tbsp (45 ml) maple syrup

½ cup (120 ml) almond milk

½ tsp vanilla extract

Ice cubes for serving, optional

To drink as a smoothie, add all the ingredients into a blender and blend until smooth. Pour the smoothie over a few ice cubes and enjoy right away.

To make popsicles, pour the mixture into a popsicle mold. Freeze the popsicles for just 30 minutes and then insert the popsicle sticks. Then, freeze the popsicles for at least 4 hours or overnight.

To remove the popsicles from the mold, run hot water over the outside of each popsicle and tug at the stick. Take care not to get any water onto the popsicle itself. Store the popsicles in a sealed container for 3 months.

Protein: 9.4 g | Fiber: 6.9 g | Fat: 21.8 g | Calories: 390 | Sodium: 136 mg | Carbs: 39.8 g | Sugars: 28.6 g

Pineapple Chocolate Magnum® Smoothie

A refreshing twist on DOLE Whip®, the trendy frozen soft serve treat that triggers lines at Disney™ parks. This sweet, tropical smoothie makes a creamy stress-reducing drink thanks to the bromelain in pineapple, which relaxes muscles and calms nerves, and magnesium-rich chocolate, which boosts the body's production of stress-reducing serotonin. Pouring it into a silicone mold, however, can transform this drink into an ice cream bar. Dip it into dark chocolate for a Klondike-bar-meets-Disney-DOLE-Whip kind of treat.

MAKES 1 (16-OZ [480-ML]) SMOOTHIE OR 8 ICE CREAM BARS

½ cup (84 g) pineapple chunks

½ cup (82 g) mango

1 cup (240 ml) coconut milk, canned

½ cup (87 g) chocolate chips, melted, for topping or for ice cream bars

Chopped nuts and coconut flakes, for ice cream bars, optional

Add the ingredients except the melted chocolate, chopped nuts and coconut flakes to a blender and process until the mixture is smooth.

To drink as a smoothie, pour the smoothie into glasses, drizzle the melted chocolate on top and enjoy right away.

To create ice cream bars, pour the mixture into molds. Freeze for 30 minutes, slip in popsicle sticks and freeze for another 4 hours or overnight.

Dip each Magnum into the melted chocolate and then place them immediately on a rack set up in the freezer. Feel free to sprinkle chopped nuts and coconut flakes on top.

Once the chocolate coating on each ice cream bar is solid, set the ice cream bars in a covered container in the freezer. Store the ice cream bars for 3 months.

Protein: 5.3 g | Fiber: 5.9 g | Fat: 38.8 g | Calories: 481 | Sodium: 19 mg | Carbs: 36.2 g | Sugars: 27.7 g

Acknowledgments

It was always my dream to share the smoothie wisdom I have accumulated over the years and to share the benefits of a daily smoothie, so creating this book is a dream come true for me. Still, the deadlines were crazy, the pressure to create was intense and the obstacles were sometimes seemingly insurmountable. So one thing is for sure, I could never have completed it without the help of a village.

My village includes so many people. The first person to thank starts with my amazing, loving and loyal husband. Philip is my creative trigger, positive voice-in-my-ear and more. A journalist and author himself, he is always saying, "It's fine, you can do it." The other endless well of support comes from my three daughters—each incredibly creative, successful and hard-working themselves. They know exactly when to push me, support me and supply ideas and they also know when to step away. And the kindness that comes from these four people on a daily basis is the main reason I feel I can accomplish anything in my life.

Another layer of support in my village comes from my incredibly supportive friends and family who tested my recipes—some many, many times. Also thank you to the smart and supportive fellow bloggers I have met on this journey. These incredible individuals help fuel my creativity and challenge me daily. And also thank you to my online village of followers. Your endless support via visits and comments motivate me to work to create the best and most delicious healthy recipes with the fewest ingredients.

Finally, up the road toward Boston is yet another arm of my village, the boundlessly energetic team at Page Street Publishing, working hand in hand with distributor Macmillan. This noteworthy publisher continues to break ground with quality publications and creative cookbooks, so I was beyond excited for the chance to create a smoothie book together. The hard-working, exceptionally talented team supported me through the creation of a smoothie book beyond my wildest dreams, despite the challenges of a pandemic buffeting us to and fro.

So much thanks and appreciation goes to my editors for their tireless and creative energy, and for helping me shape my book with laser-sharp precision on meaning, message and accuracy. And a huge thank-you to the design team for their out-of-the-box thinking and professional skill in creating a package that truly represents what I wanted to share.

About the Author

Dee Dine is the creator of Green Smoothie Gourmet, a popular healthy food blog where she shares smoothie recipes—as well as desserts and meals—that are nutritious, easy to prepare, plant-based and typically require only a few familiar ingredients.

Dee is also the parfait editor with feedfeed, an online cooking consortium, and has been published by BuzzFeed, mindbodygreen, Well + Good, *Marie Claire* and *Thrive* magazine, and her healthy, easy recipes have been shared by countless publications and brands on social media. She may have a graduate degree in the sciences, but friends say one of her greatest talents is hiding vegetables in unsuspecting recipes.

Follow her on Instagram @greensmoothiegourmet. For more healthy and minimal ingredient recipes, go to greensmoothiegourmet.com.

Index